IMAGES
of America
EL MONTE

ON THE COVER: Kauffman Mercantile Company was the first general store in El Monte. Pictured are several modes of transportation, c. 1911.

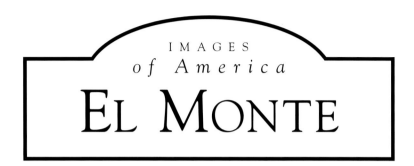

IMAGES of America
EL MONTE

Jorane King Barton
El Monte Historical Society

Copyright © 2006 by Jorane King Barton and the El Monte Historical Society
ISBN 978-0-7385-4652-0

Published by Arcadia Publishing
Charleston SC, Chicago IL, Portsmouth NH, San Francisco CA

Printed in the United States of America

Library of Congress Catalog Card Number: 2006924394

For all general information contact Arcadia Publishing at:
Telephone 843-853-2070
Fax 843-853-0044
E-mail sales@arcadiapublishing.com
For customer service and orders:
Toll-Free 1-888-313-2665

Visit us on the Internet at www.arcadiapublishing.com

Contents

Acknowledgments   6

Introduction   7

1.   A Village Is Born   9

2.   Law and Order: Monte Boys Style   53

3.   The School   61

4.   The Lion Farm: A Roaring Success   77

5.   El Monte in the 20th Century   89

ACKNOWLEDGMENTS

Researching the material and photographs of El Monte has been very nostalgic for us who grew up here. In the 1920s, the town was surrounded by farms, walnut groves, and vacant lots filled with wild mustard and radish. Many homes had their own vegetable gardens and rabbit hutches to provide food for the family. As children, we climbed the trees and played among the wild flowers.

This area was settled in 1851 by a group of pioneers from Iowa, known as the Thompson Party. They were joined in 1852 by the Johnson Party from Lexington, Kentucky. In setting foot on the land by both the Rio Hondo and San Gabriel Rivers, they began the development of the community known as El Monte.

El Monte was a thriving town in the 1930s and 1940s. Every Saturday night, the citizenry would turn out on Main Street. We had a movie theater, a drugstore with soda fountain, a 5 and 10¢ store, a root-beer parlor, a pool hall, a Market Basket grocery store, a tailor, and several highly fashionable clothing emporiums. Long gone and mostly forgotten were the Shoshonean Indians who once roamed the land.

Today the inhabitants residing in this ever-growing city are either descendents of the early pioneers who first came to El Monte or settlers from other parts of the nation and world.

The history now resides in the El Monte Historical Museum. I would like to thank the current curator, Donna Crippen, Virginia Mosely, and the other volunteers for the meticulous work they do to make this museum attractive and meaningful. I would also like to thank the previous curator, Lillian Wiggins, as her work set the stage for what we see in the museum today. The City of El Monte deserves our appreciation for all their support. I would like to thank my late husband, Jack Barton, former El Monte High School principal, for his loving admiration of his adopted hometown. His two books made me and many others appreciative of the life we had growing up in El Monte. And lastly, I have to mention my daughter, Nancy Body, the computer expert. She always comes to my rescue.

Introduction

In 1851, a group of weary travelers crossed the San Gabriel River and found a fertile tract of land, which promised an abundance of agricultural possibilities. This group of parched pioneers was the Thompson Party, a small band of families from Muscatine, Iowa. They left their homes in answer to the siren call of the California gold fields. Little did they know what an arduous journey they had undertaken. What they were faced with were hundreds and hundreds of miles of barren Arizona terrain as they crossed one desert after another. Their constant thirst forced them to alter their objectives and instead of seeking the gold fields, their ambitions now became simply to settle wherever they could find a place that afforded a continuous source of fresh water and sufficient arable land for the growing of crops. They found these conditions as they forded the San Gabriel River and stepped onto land where they began the development of the permanent community know today as El Monte.

Within a year, a second party of thirsty pioneers crossed the San Gabriel River about a mile north of the Thompson ford. This band was known as the Johnson Party, named for their leader, Captain Johnson, from Lexington, Kentucky. After crossing the San Gabriel, Captain Johnson led his followers several miles to the west. There he found the Rio Hondo River, a small branch of the San Gabriel, which would offer his party a source of fresh water. In coming west, the Johnson Party had suffered the same sort of hardships and deprivation as the Thompson Party. Johnson's group also set the same pact as the Thompson Party, which was to stop and settle at the first site that afforded an abundant supply of fresh water and opportunity to till the soil.

Captain Johnson's group established a campsite just a short distance east of the Rio Hondo River. Meanwhile, the Thompson camp had situated themselves somewhat east of where their group had forded the San Gabriel River. The distance separating the two campsites was less than two miles as the crow flies.

The proximity of the two groups engendered friendliness, cooperation, and mutual activities of work or pleasure. Before long, there was a general sense of community shared by all, and they began to think of themselves as a village.

At the same time, the stature of Captain Johnson grew in both camps. His skills and knowledge were much respected by all and his prestige grew day by day. When asked if his title of captain was real or honorary, the villagers learned that as a young man he had fought in several Appalachian Indian wars and had been awarded the rank of captain for his bravery and leadership in these backwoods campaigns. Without a vote or an appointment, Captain Johnson was readily recognized by all as the leader of their village. Out of the universal respect that they felt for their leader, the two camps of pioneers mutually agreed to name their village Lexington in honor of their foremost citizen, a Kentuckian.

The name Lexington was used for many years—until 1866 to be exact. In that year, the state legislature divided California into townships, and each township was given a name. Lexington's township was named in honor of the old Spanish name bestowed on the area by the Spanish expedition of Capt. General de Portola in 1771. In the Spanish spoken at that time, the term El Monte could be translated as "the wooded place."

The town of Lexington was designated by the legislature to be the capitol of the township of El Monte. This decision stirred the people of Lexington. Some wanted to retain the town name that been selected by their pioneers. Others argued that the town should acquire the more ancient name of El Monte to be in line with the newly named township. After much discussion and debate, a vote was held and the name of the town was changed from Lexington to El Monte.

El Monte was the first purely American settlement in the vicinity of what is now Los Angeles County. El Monte also had the first Protestant church organized in the state and one of the very first public schools in California. It became the country's largest walnut producer, as well as the hops capitol of the United States. It was also known for the unique lion farm, which drew visitors from the surrounding area and across the country. Things have changed since the early 1850s, but a reminder of those courageous pioneers is on the streets, schools, buildings, and of course, in the El Monte Historical Museum.

One

A Village Is Born

In 1841, ranchers John Rowland and William Workman led the first American wagon trains into the San Gabriel Mission area. Vast acres of land were deeded to them by Gov. Pio Pico. Early observers told of wild cattle and horses swarming all over the ranches. After hearing of the successful cattle business and the California gold rush, many others determined to come to this land of opportunity.

With the arrival of the Thompson Party in 1851 and the Johnson Party in 1852, a lively community developed, consisting of no more than a dozen small families. The villagers vigorously began to build their community—erecting schools, farming the land, establishing businesses, and making their new homes as much like the communities they had left behind as possible.

The following description of this bustling village was made by a party of government engineers:

> Having crossed the little river of San Gabriel, we reached the precincts of the town of Monte. Each spot of 160 acres for miles in all directions appeared to be ditched around, hedged and cultivated. Houses of canvas, brush, boards, or of adobe gave shelter to families of settlers. Improvements were rapidly progressing. There were the cheerful sounds of American voices, blacksmith's hammer, and the merry laugh of children trudging to school. The whole scene appeared very odd, as if by magic, a New England village had sprung up upon the Pacific. Their estimate of the fertility of the soil and the excellence of the climate is exhibited by their leaving rich placers to cultivate and improve land.

Thriving industries sprang up. El Monte became known for the hops they grew, for the produce grown on their farms, and for the many dairies that thrived in the area. A broom factory made 50 brooms a day. Colorful flowers grown for their seed covered acres of land, and people came from miles around to view the scene. El Monte bacon graced the tables of many kitchens. Even walnuts grew in bountiful amounts and were sent nationwide. The villagers were successful with their products.

El Monte had arrived and was here to stay.

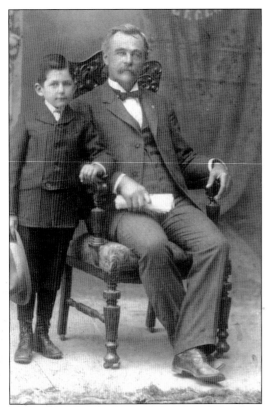

George B. Renfro was a Civil War veteran having fought under General Sherman. He came to El Monte in 1885 and bought a farm a mile or two west of the Rio Hondo Bridge. He was initiated into the Masonic fraternity in 1869 and became one of the early members of Lexington Lodge No. 104, F&AM. He lived to be almost 100 years old and served the community with honor and esteem. His daughter was Della Gidley, wife of pioneer Seth Gidley and mother of George Gidley, the rancher for whom Gidley School is named. Renfro was the first public weigh master in this district, continuing in that capacity for over 50 years at the same location on Valley Boulevard. The weigh station recently closed after 117 years of continuous service. Below he and his wife, Martha, relax beside a rose brush noted for having 29 varieties of roses grafted on it.

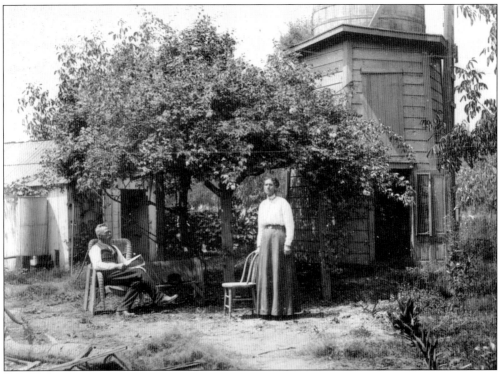

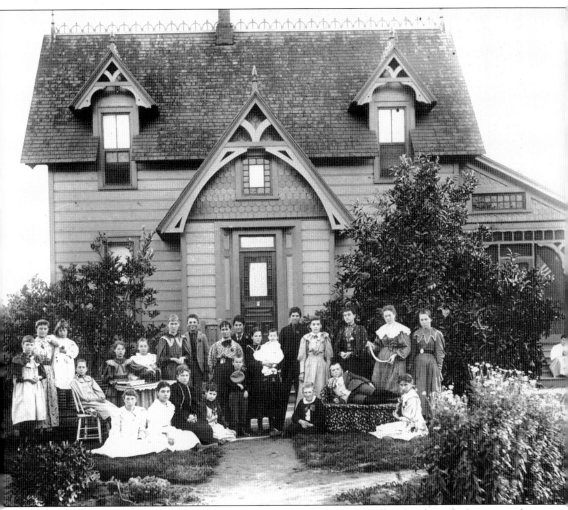

Martha Renfro and her offspring are in front of their home on Valley Boulevard. George and Martha had one son and three daughters. Daughter Etta married a Seth DeGarmo and Della married George Gidley, both well-known members of the community. Martha Renfro died in 1930 shortly after she and George celebrated their 68th wedding anniversary.

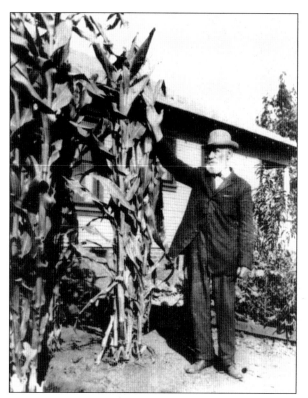

Seth Gidley proudly displays the tall corn grown in the rich soil of El Monte. Not only did vegetables grow in great abundance, the fertile land was responsible for the hops, flower fields, willows, and other greenery that made El Monte the envy of other towns or "the garden city of the valley."

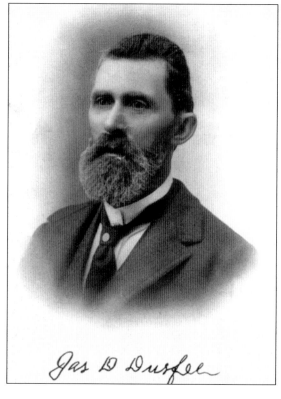

James Durfee (1858–1920) was a successful rancher and walnut grower. He brought the first purebred cattle to El Monte, initiating a dairy industry that grew into 66 local dairies. Durfee Road and Durfee School are named after him.

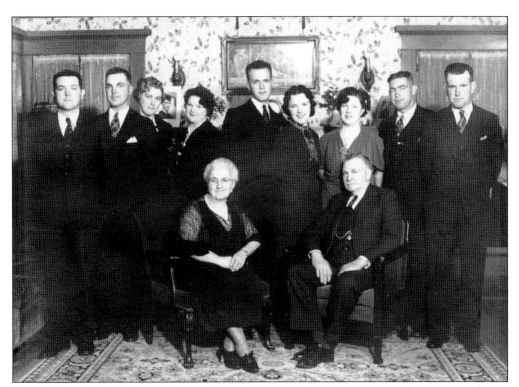

Pictured here is the family of James R. Durfee, son of pioneer James D. Durfee, a successful rancher and realtor. James and his wife, Estelle, along with Miles, Olen, Ruth, Mildred, Glen, Eva, Alle, James, and Hillard are all gathered here.

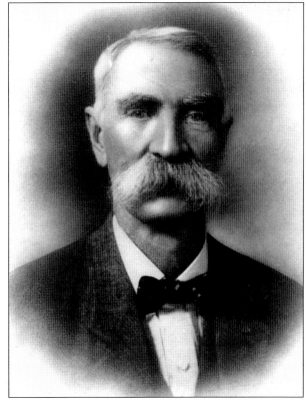

James Cleminson was born in 1833 in Independence, Missouri. He traveled by wagon train to El Monte in 1852 with his family. His son, James D. Cleminson, was a partner with A. N. Wiggins in general contracting. They owned a livery business and installed the first public water system in El Monte. James D., the son, was also a successful farmer and dairyman.

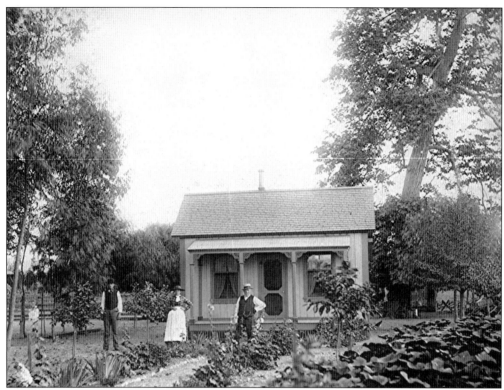

John Allgeyer, his wife, and son Henry are pictured here. He came to California in 1881, purchased 16 acres of new land, and planted walnut trees. His homestead was also planted with lush vegetation consisting of tobacco and hops.

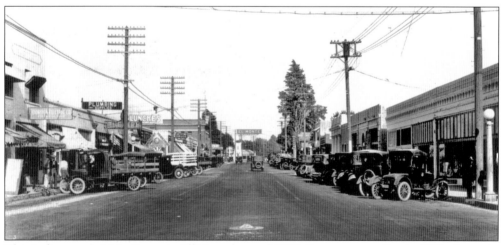

This is downtown Main Street in El Monte around 1908. Forty years earlier, in 1860, the main towns in Los Angeles County were the dusty pueblo of Los Angeles and the American village of El Monte. At that time, El Monte was depicted as a raw frontier town populated by a band of vigilantes known as the Monte Boys, who recklessly defended justice.

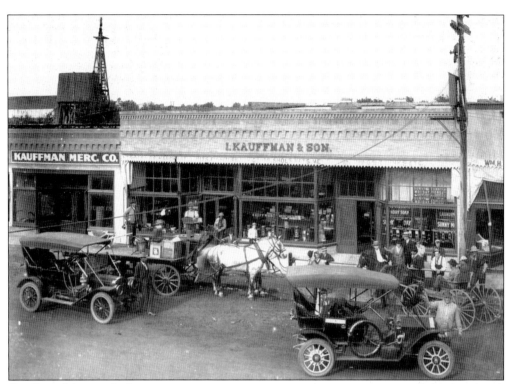

Kauffman Mercantile Company was the first general store in El Monte. In this c. 1911 photograph are several modes of transportation.

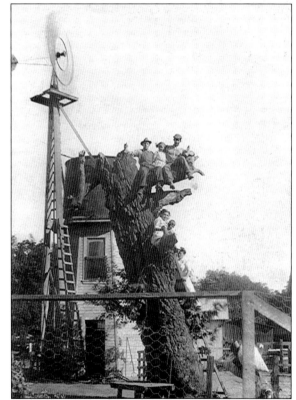

Before a water district was established in 1913, each resident had his own well, and many used windmills to pump the water and run grain mills. Pictured here is the windmill and tank house at the old Allgeyer home.

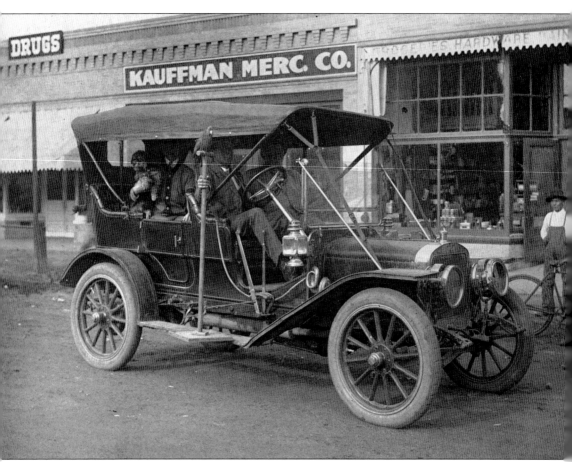

Irving Kauffman's Pope Hartford automobile is parked in front of the store in 1911. Note the parrot on the pole and the dog, both pets of Mr. Kauffman, the owner of the mercantile company. The Irving Kauffman was the shopping hub of El Monte in the early 1900s. Not only did it offer the necessary provisions for the town folk, one could also be entertained with the latest cars and also his menagerie.

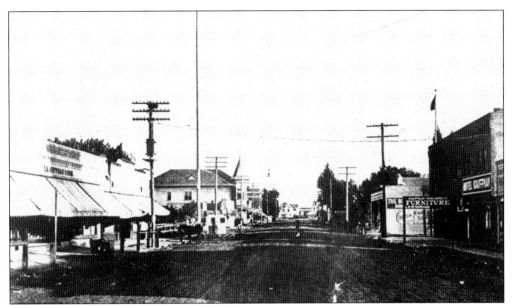
This street scene shows some of the same landmarks as those seen in 1908 and 1914.

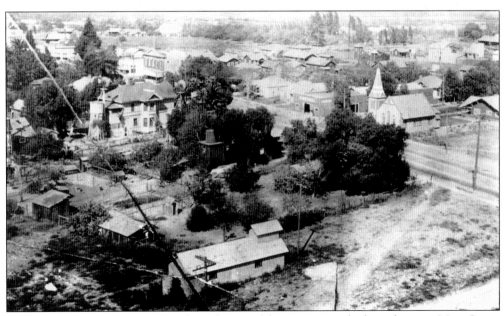
El Monte is pictured here, c. 1914, from the top of the water tower looking down on Main Street and Tyler Avenue.

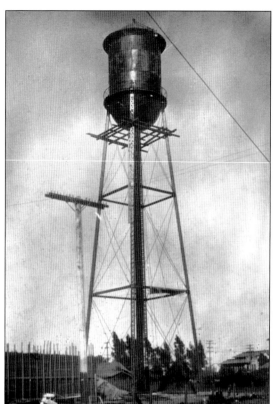

The city water tower was not only a recognizable beacon of El Monte but also had a light and siren to alert the police or firemen to emergencies.

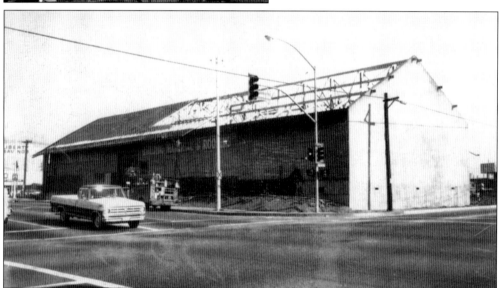

In 1868, J. R. Durfee planted the first grove of walnuts. In 1888, B. F. Maxson and P. F. Cogswell purchased land and began the first large-scale planting of walnuts. In 1920, more than 4,000 acres were in production. The walnut growers formed an organization in 1896 to set prices and terms. Walnut growing began to decline in the late 1920s, due in part to disease, the Depression, high taxes, and land values. The packinghouse pictured here was on the east side of Tyler Avenue across the street from the Pacific Electric Railroad station.

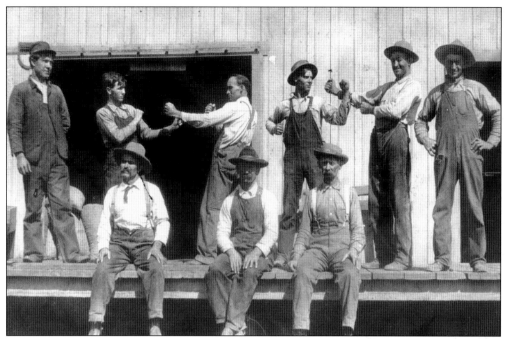

Local boys practice fisticuffs at the walnut-packing plant in El Monte, the walnut-growing capital of the world, c. 1895. Included are Maxon, Pearson, Percy, Albert Freer, Ed Fawcett, Walter Freer, Jeff Thurman, and Bill Thurman.

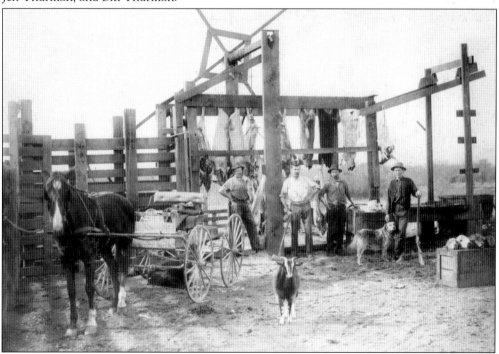

The first slaughterhouse in El Monte was in operation in 1895. Located across the Southern Pacific tracks on the banks of the Rio Hondo River, it was operated by William Knott, the man on the right. He is accompanied by a goat and his dog Shep.

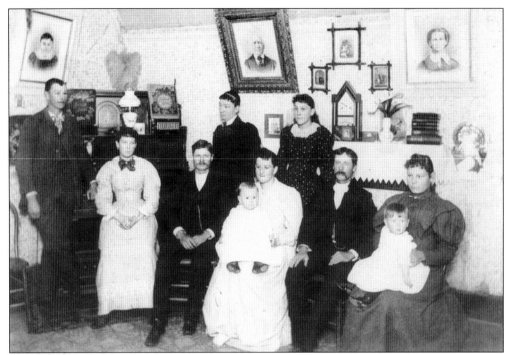

The Schmidt and Freer families gather together to pose for this photograph. Pictured, from left to right, are (first row) Jack Freer, Camilla Schmidt, Lee Freer, Jane Schmidt Freer with baby, Tom Freer, and Victoria Schmidt Freer with baby; (second row) Eliza Schmidt and Consuela Schmidt.

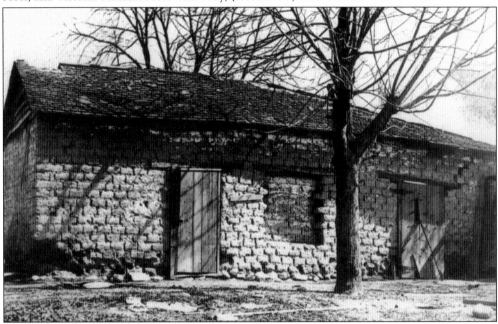

The Schmidt adobe home, probably the earliest dwelling built in El Monte, was located on Valley Boulevard not far from Gay's Lion Farm. Nicholas Schmidt, who arrived by wagon train in the early 1850s, erected the house. He was the village smithy and established a blacksmith shop on Main Street.

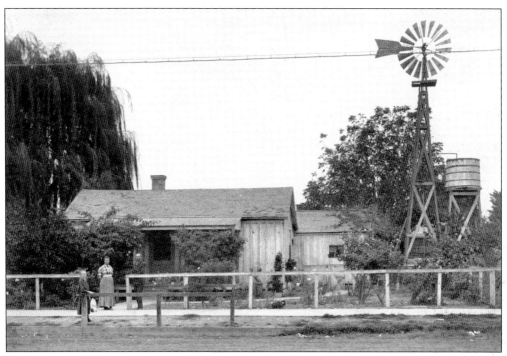

Frank Magee and Camilla Schmidt were born in this house located on Main Street.

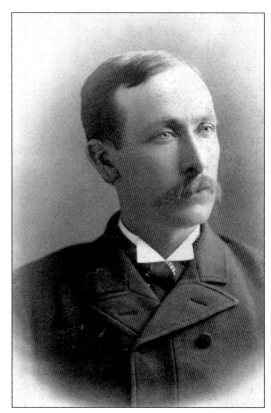

Dr. Frederick Payson Cave came to El Monte in 1888. He immediately began to practice medicine and, in due time, built up a large practice. He was extremely active in the establishment of a high school in El Monte and served on the board of trustees for years.

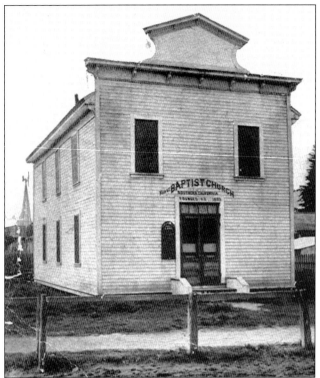

As soon as the early pioneers settled, they established the First Baptist Church, founded in 1853. In 1852, church services were held in the Willow Schoolhouse under the leadership of Rev. J. A. Johnson.

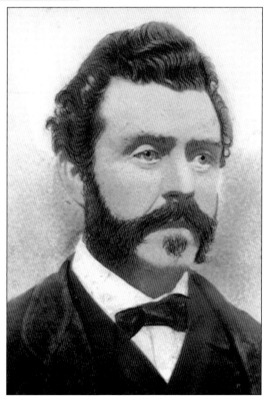

J. N. Cecil, a saloon keeper in El Monte, kept busy in the late 1800s. Besides dispensing liquor, he had to schedule meetings in his building.

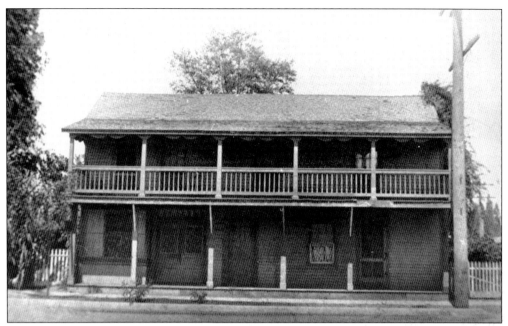

The Old Cecil Saloon and the early Masonic Lodge Building are pictured here in 1855. El Monte had the third Masonic Lodge in Southern California, organized in 1855. The charter was granted in 1856. A separate lodge hall was built in 1907 for Lexington Lodge No. 194.

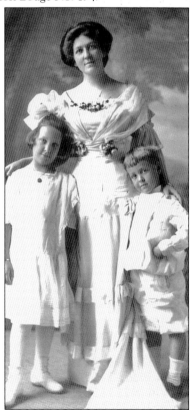

Lovely Margaret J. Schmidt stands here with her two children.

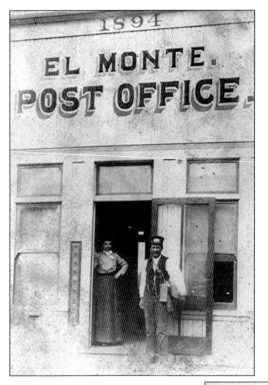

This was the U.S. Post Office in 1894. Ira Thompson, the first wagon master to bring pioneers to El Monte, served as the first postmaster. Earlier the Butterfield Overland Mail stage service made regular one-way trips from St. Louis, Missouri, in about 18 days. Looking for faster service, the Pony Express was established. In 1869, a transcontinental railway service took the place of the Pony Express.

Prescott Cogswell, a well-known El Monte pioneer, served as a member of the California State Assembly, a state senator, and later as a member of the Los Angeles County Board of Supervisors. Cogswell School, Cogswell Avenue, and Cogswell Dam and Reservoir are named after him.

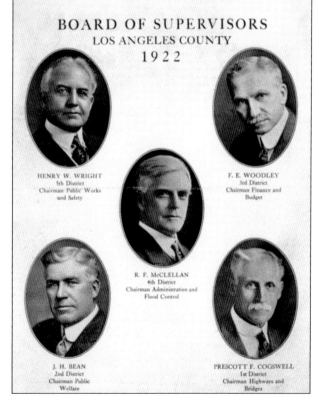

Born in Scotland, William Elliott came to El Monte in 1883 as superintendent of four ranches owned by E. J. (Lucky) Baldwin. In 1887, he resigned to tend to his vast walnut grove. He was considered a master of walnut cultivation and was one of the organizers of the Walnut Growers Association.

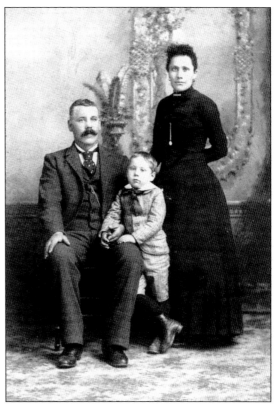

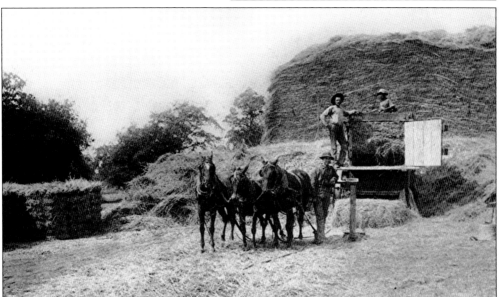

A successful farmer, Tom Wiggins purchased 18 acres of land on Peck Road, east of the town. The land was planted with walnut trees, which he removed before planting alfalfa. Here he is pictured baling hay in 1910. When he was younger, he was famous jockey, having won races in the cross-country steeplechase in Pasadena, which always followed the Tournament of Roses Parade. He also was an expert driver in the chariot races.

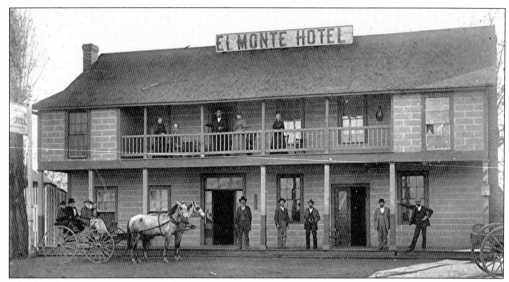

The hotels in El Monte assumed many names and owners. In 1870, W. L. Jones built this hotel and named it the El Monte Hotel. It was located on Granada Avenue and Main Street. In 1875, W. R. Dodson bought the hotel, which then became known as the Lexington Hotel, from W. C. Martin.

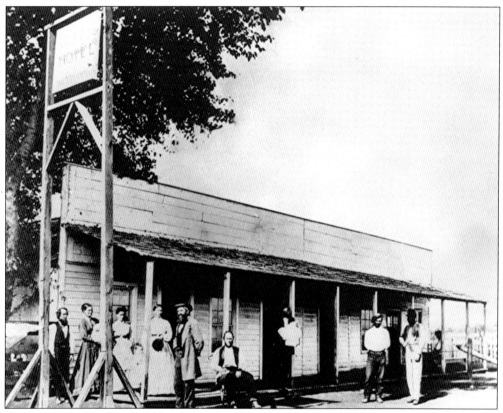

The Lexington Hotel looked like this in the 1870s. Comparing it with prior photograph, one can see that improvements have been made to the establishment.

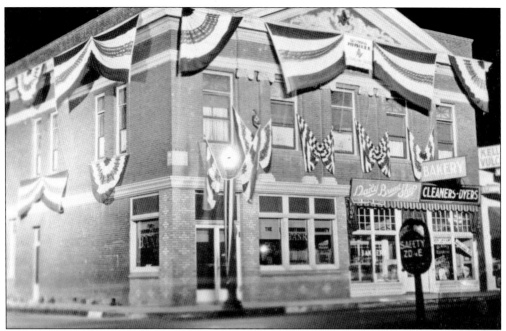

The Dodson Building is pictured here in full regalia celebrating Independence Day.

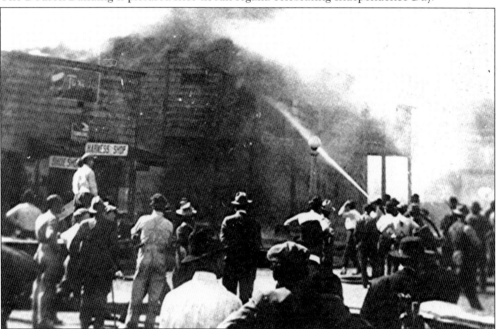

The Dodson Hotel, to which Mr. Dodson had made many improvements, burned in 1916. In addition to owning the hotel, Dodson was involved in many enterprises, including the Dodson Hall, a two-story building; a livery stable; a farm; and several rental cottages. In his farm operations, he devoted considerable attention to improved stock. His cattle were Jersey and short-horned Durham breeds. Among his horses were two fine stallions of Belmont stock. For 50 years, he was a resident of the beautiful San Gabriel Valley and a prominent contributor to the community of El Monte.

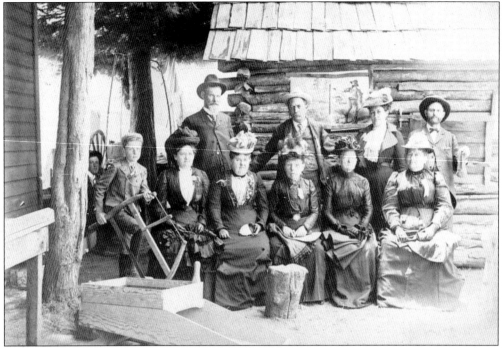

The Dodson family enjoys an outing with others. William Dodson is standing to the left, Clara Jones Dodson is seated in front of him, and Foster Dodson is the boy with the bucksaw.

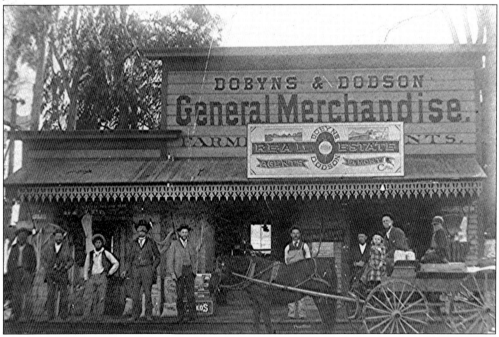

These two men, George Dobyns and William Dodson, became business partners in the late 1890s. They opened the Dobyns and Dodson General Merchandise and Real Estate Office, one of the first general stores in El Monte, located on Main Street near Granada Avenue. They did not have the business long as Dobyns died in 1898.

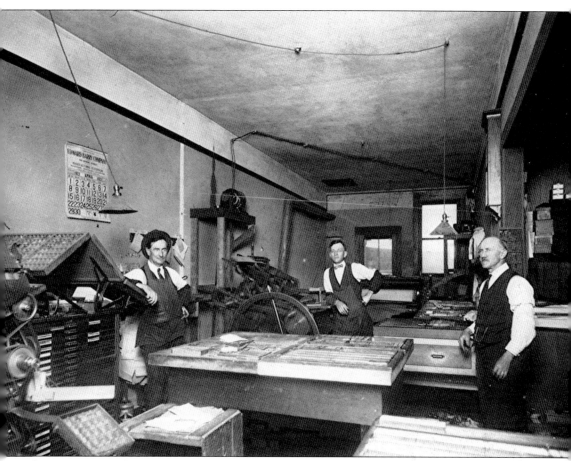

El Monte Gazette, El Monte's first newspaper, proudly displays its linotype machine. Mr. Maltman, right, was the editor. In 1906, Maltman sold the *El Monte Gazette* to C. N. Whitaker. In 1923, the name of the paper was changed to the *El Monte Herald,* and Neil R. Murray became the new editor and publisher.

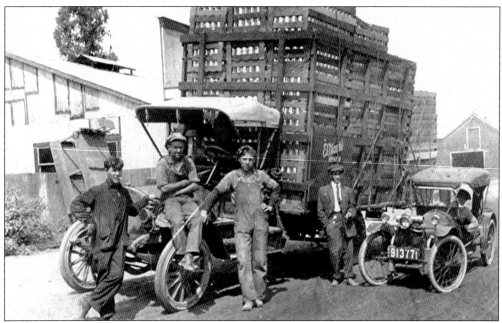

The El Monte Cannery was near Main Street and Granada Avenue behind the Public Market, c. 1915. The locals shopped there as they could buy dented cans of fruit at a discount. It closed around 1930.

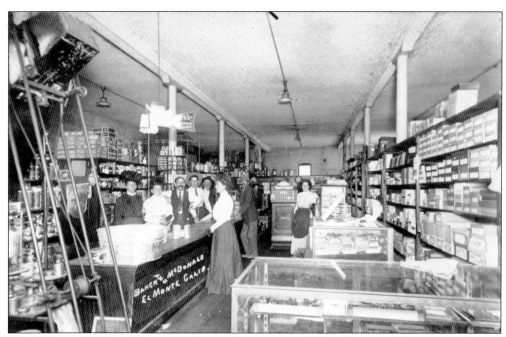

The Baker and McDonald store on the southeast corner of Main Street and Lexington Avenue sold general merchandise. Pictured, from left to right, are Mrs. John Lowery, Mrs. Henry Rhode, Henry Rhode, Fred McDonald, and two unidentified men. Mrs. Osmond is in front of the counter and Josie Ritter is on the far right.

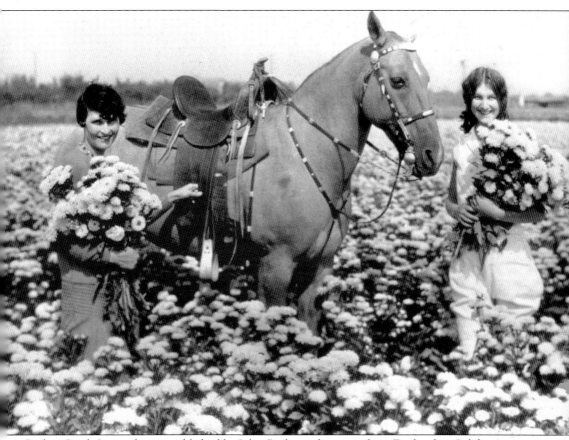

Bodger Seeds Limited was established by John Bodger, who came from England to California in 1890. He and his brother Tom started this business in Gardena with a sweet-pea farm. In 1916, recognizing that El Monte had the ideal microclimate for certain flowers, the company began purchasing land. By 1924, there were over 1,000 acres of flowers. They distributed seeds to 50 different countries. It was quite a sight to see acres of variously colored flowers blooming. Visitors came from near and far to gaze upon these spectacularly colored fields.

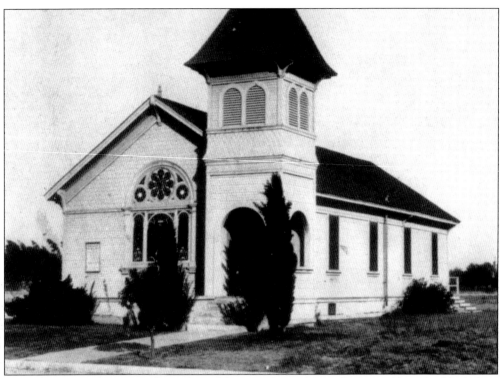
The Episcopal church, a small wooden edifice, was beautiful inside. It was located a block from Columbia Grammar School on Columbia Street. Many young El Monteans were married there.

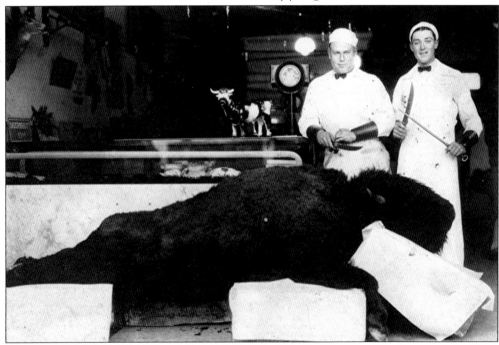
Walter Freer butchers a buffalo while teaching Babe Johnson the art of butchering at the Freer Meat Market in 1910. Walter and his brother Tommy, the local dentist, served in World War I.

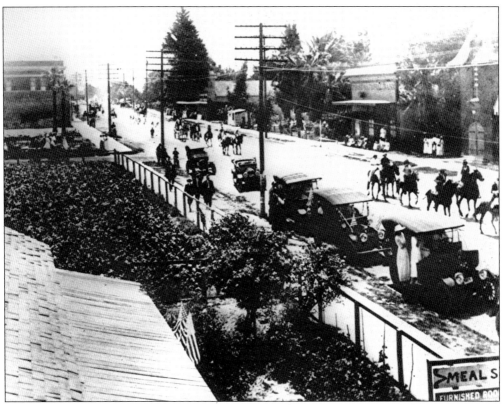
This 1912 Fourth of July parade celebrated both the birth of the nation and the incorporation of El Monte. El Monteans loved parades, especially patriotic ones.

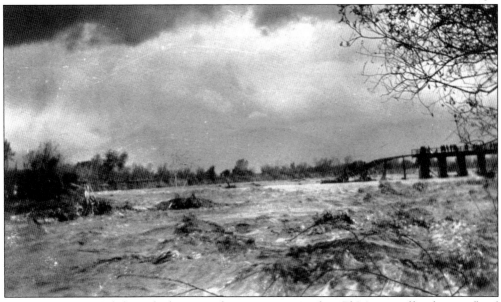
Raging waters roared through the rivers during stormy weather. El Monte suffered many flood disasters until the dams were built in San Gabriel Canyon. One dam was named after Prescott Cogswell, an early pioneer.

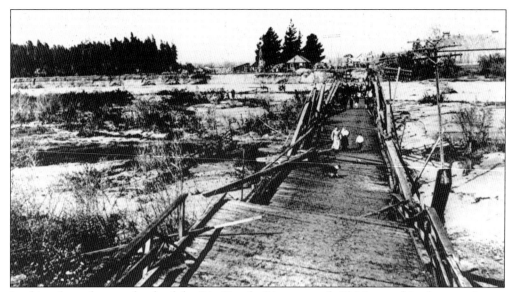

Looking from the west bank of the Rio Hondo River towards El Monte, this photograph was taken in 1914. In 1868, an article in the *Los Angeles News* told about the Rio Hondo during a heavy storm:

> At the Monte, through which a portion of the San Gabriel runs, the stream has assumed the proportions of a real river and gone wild, cutting its channel by washing many acres of land, houses, fine fruit trees, vines, etc., which were the sole support of many families. Often after heavy rains, this stream, known as the Rio Hondo, would come as far as the Monte, and then would spread out over much space south of town, but never did much damage.

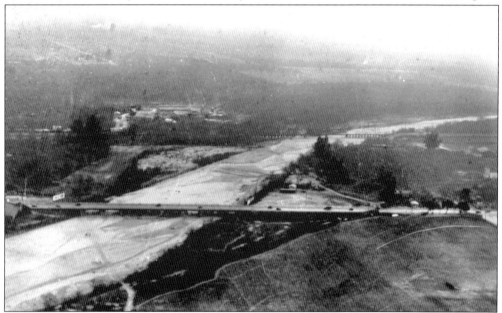

The peaceful Rio Hondo River on a cloudy day is quite a contrast to the stormy days, which caused harmful floods and uncertainty among the citizens as to whether they should stay in El Monte or move to higher ground.

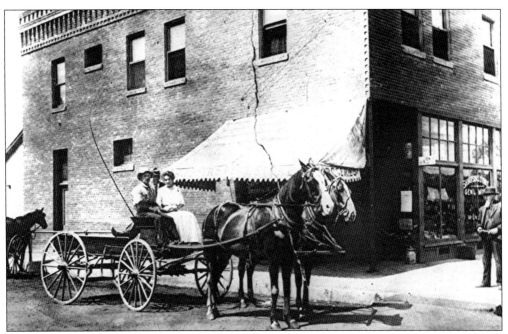

Ephriam J. Shirpser, owner of this store, was a native Californian who worked a year for Kauffman Mercantile Company. He then opened a plumbing business with Lester Burdick for two years before going into partnership with his father opening a general store.

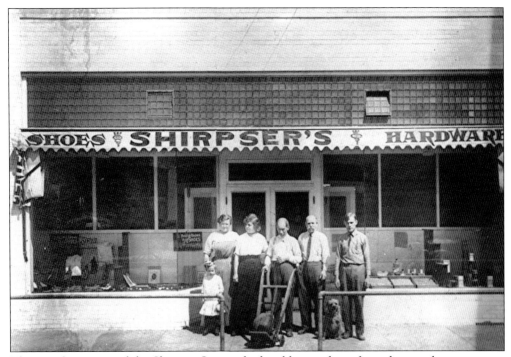

This is a front view of the Shirpser Store, which sold everything from shoes to housewares to hardware. Having tried several occupations, Ephriam soon left commerce and became a real estate and insurance agent.

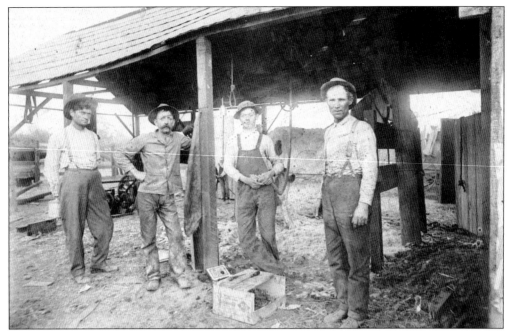

John Broaded is standing on the right in one of El Monte's blacksmith shops. There were several blacksmith shops in town with different owners up through the 1930s. Prow Leffler owned one on Valley Boulevard across from the lion farm. His wife, Nellie Leffler, became mayor and championed gambling in the town.

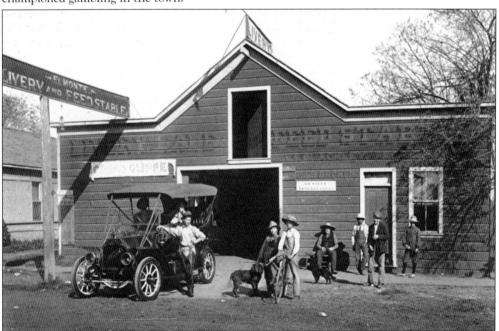

This blacksmith shop, located on the southwest corner of Valley Boulevard and Granada Avenue, burned in 1925. Blacksmith shops were numerous in El Monte. Horses were not only a means of transportation, they were a necessity for farming, ranching, hauling, and horse racing. Blacksmith shops also made tools, fences, chains, and horseshoes.

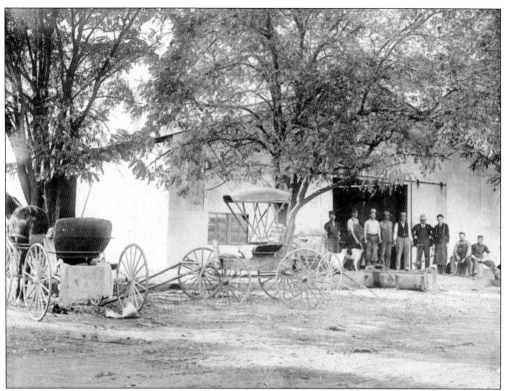

The Burdick blacksmith shop was located on the southwest corner of Granada Avenue and Main Street. A new structure was erected after a fire destroyed the original shop. Burdick was in business from 1889 until 1911. Horses needed tending, not only work horses but racing horses also. There was a racetrack in El Monte, and in the 1870s, Lucky Baldwin built a track at what is now the county golf course in nearby Arcadia. Horse races were held on Main Street, and crowds gathered to watch.

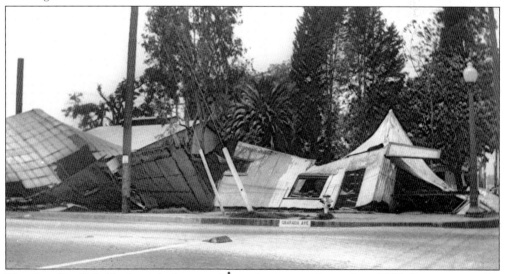

The first Burdick blacksmith shop on Granada Avenue burned in 1925. One can see the total devastation.

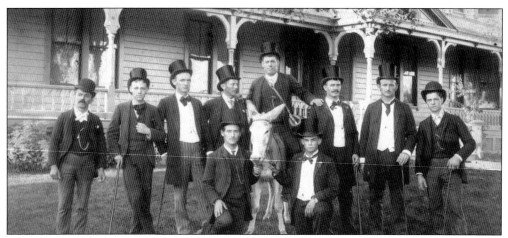
Jockeys from Lucky Baldwin's ranch pose around 1880 with El Montean Archie Wiggins sitting on the donkey.

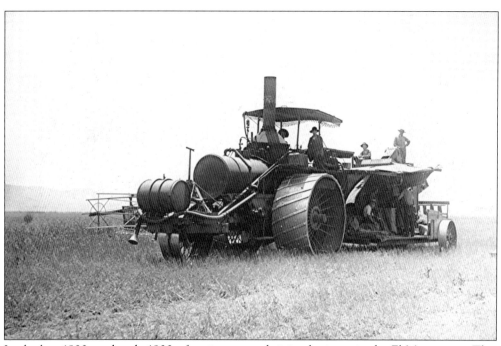
In the late 1800s and early 1900s, farming was a thriving business in the El Monte area. This thrashing machine is being used where Whittier Narrows Dam is today.

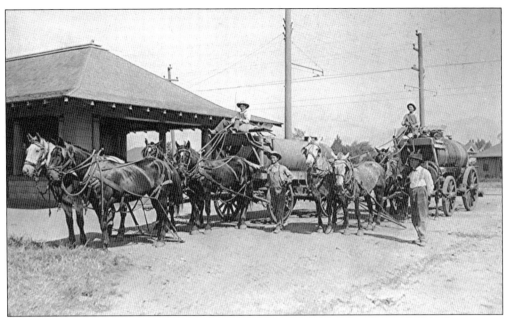

Henry W. Thienes and his working road crew are at the old Pacific Electric railroad station on Tyler Avenue. The Southern Pacific Railroad opened a station in this same area in 1874.

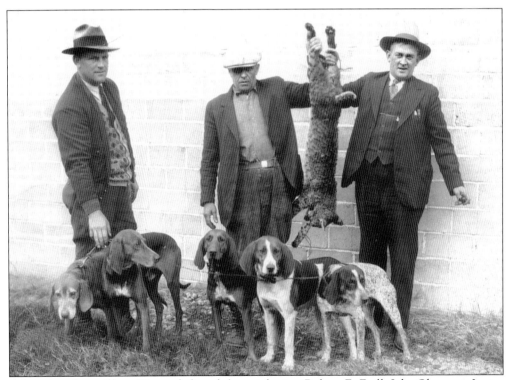

A hunting they will go. Pictured, from left to right, are Robert E. Faell, Jake Obancon, Lester Burdick, and their dogs Traveler, Kelly, Daisy, unidentified, and Chip. Jake and Lester are holding the catch, a subdued bobcat.

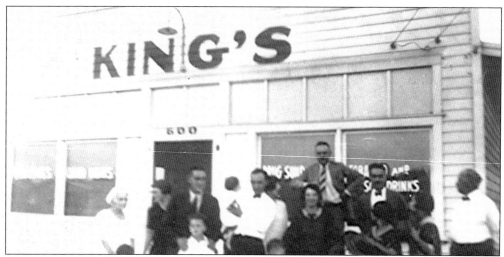

Kings Grocery Store was originally owned by Louis King. He was the father of Fred King, pictured third from the left, who later served many terms as El Monte mayor. Another son, Stoddard King, pictured second from right, was the lyricist for Long, Long Trail A-winding, a song popular during World War I. This photograph was taken in 1920, and the store is now operating under the name of La Tienita.

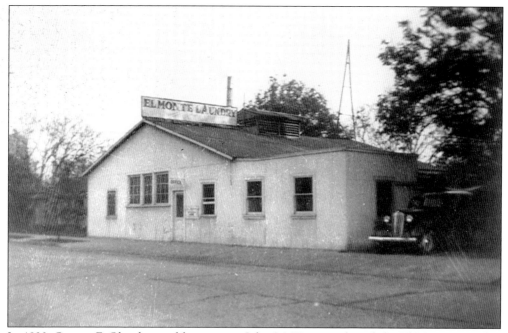

In 1930, George F. Glandon and his partner John McNeer purchased the El Monte Laundry. The washing was done in the garage and ironing was done on the lower floor of the house. The equipment consisted of two wooden washers, an extractor with a load capacity of a small wash tub, two electric hand irons, a homemade tumbler drier, a gas-fired mangle, and a 10-horsepower boiler about the size of a large domestic water heater. The boiler was filled by means of a hand pump. In 1931, Glandon bought his partner's interest and moved the laundry to the corner of Tyler Avenue and Kauffman Street. His children, Kenneth and Eugene, modernized the building and equipment in 1944.

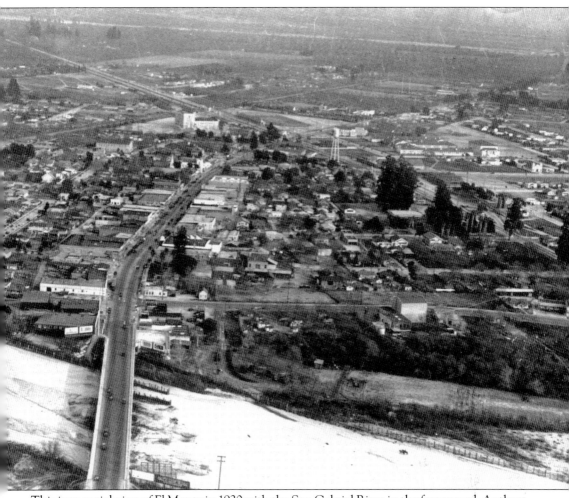
This is an aerial view of El Monte in 1920 with the San Gabriel River in the foreground. As these pictures progress, one can also see the activity in the town's growth. The recognizable beacon of El Monte, the water tower stands tall in the background.

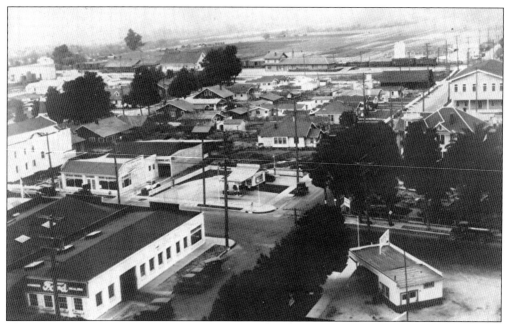

This view of the city was taken in 1925 from the water tower on Tyler Avenue near the fire station and police department. It had a light on top that would illuminate when the telephone rang. The policeman on duty could see it from any part of town and respond immediately. The tower also had a siren on it to call the volunteer firemen in case of fire.

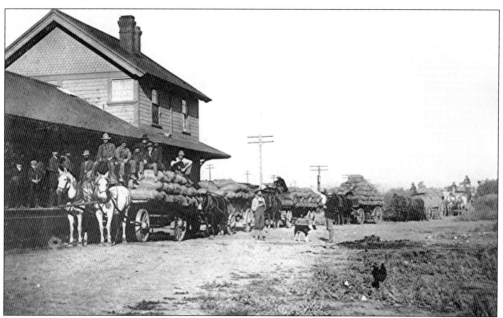

In 1873, the Southern Pacific Company began work building railroads. In 1874, El Monte's first depot opened, and on April 24, the first trains ran through El Monte. Sacks of produce are being loaded onto the Southern Pacific railroad in the Bassett area.

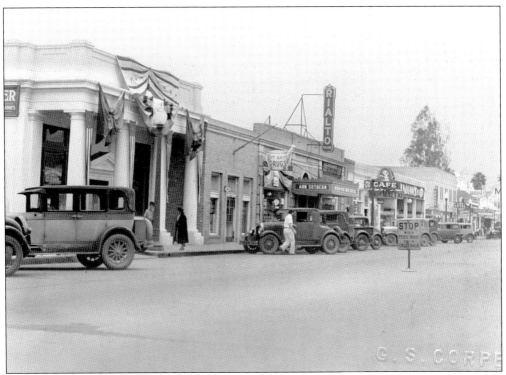

The Rialto Theatre in El Monte was the first theater owned and run by Arthur Sanborn. It was located on the south side of Main Street. The El Monte Chamber of Commerce had a room upstairs where they conducted business. Other associations also held meetings there.

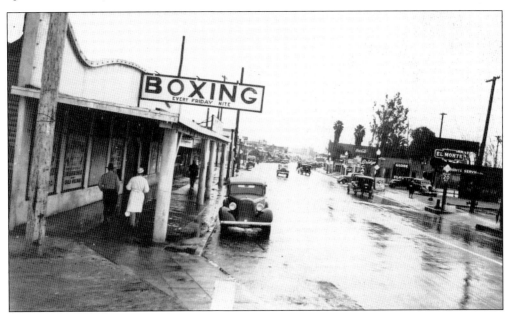

This is the scene on Main Street looking east from the bridge during a rainstorm in 1933. On the left is the old Swanee River Dance Hall, a swinging hangout years ago. It was rebuilt later and again became very popular.

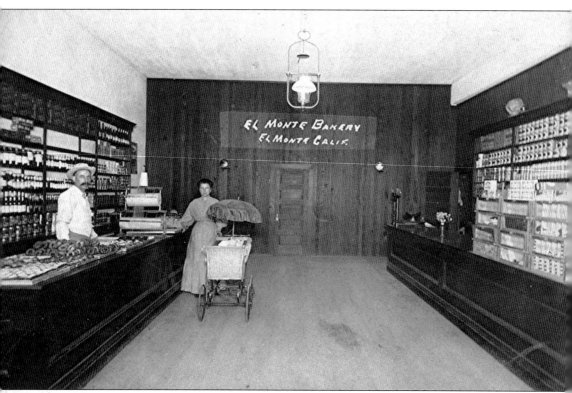

In 1903, Harry Woods opened the El Monte Bakery, renamed Woods Bakery, on Main Street. One of El Monte's oldest established businesses, it served the population for over 50 years.

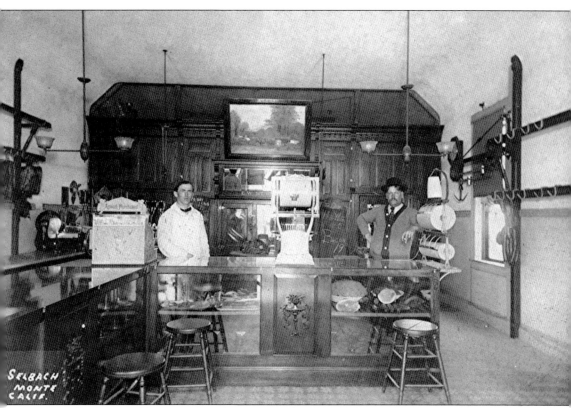

E. W. Selbach opened his very up-to-date meat market on Main Street, across the street from J. C. Penney, in 1900. It became a popular, thriving business, and with the profits, he built a number of business buildings on Main Street, which is now Valley Boulevard. He served for 14 years on the city council and was an original stockholder of the First National Bank of El Monte.

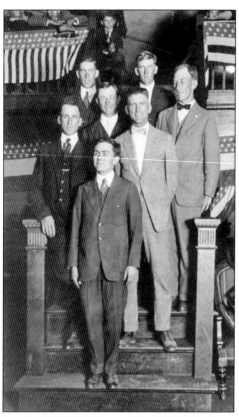

In 1914, El Monte men leave home for World War I. Included in this photograph are Guy McMichael, John Guess, Gerbert Cortez, Del Steers, Mr. Shell, Mr. Hamlin, and Fred Rush.

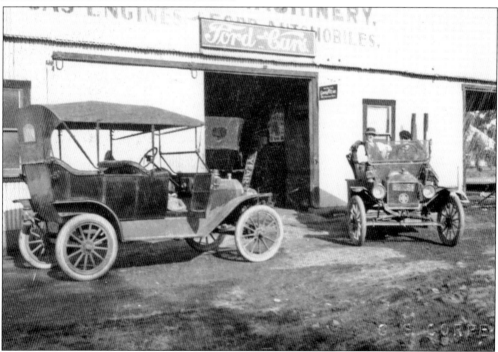

In 1914, the front of the Ford Garage faced Granada Avenue.

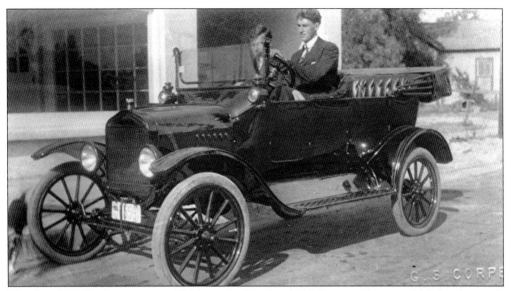
The first 1917 Ford car came to El Monte in October 1916. Barney Corpe and his brother were instrumental in bringing these cars to town.

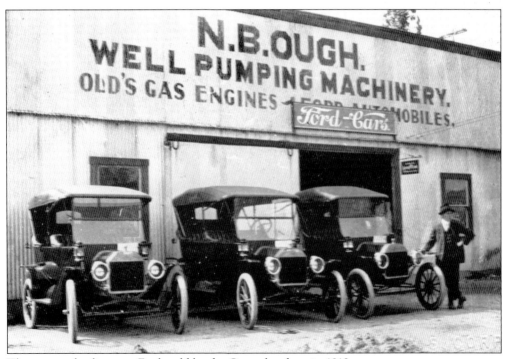
These were the first new Fords sold by the Corpe brothers in 1918.

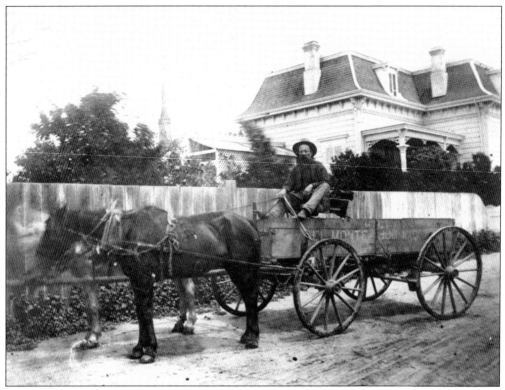

The El Monte Transfer Company began in the early days and stayed in business for many years.

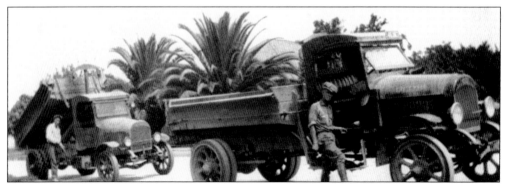

During the 1920s and 1930s, Consolidated Rock and Gravel Company was a source of work for many in El Monte. This photograph portrays Bud and Ed Milllan.

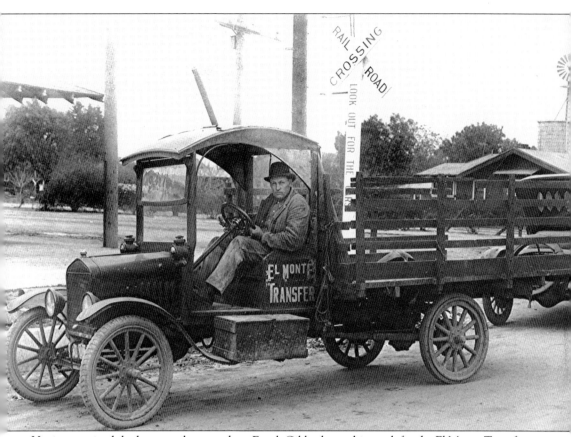
Having survived the horse-and-wagon days, Frank Gibbs drove this truck for the El Monte Transfer Company in the 1920s. He later became the high school custodian.

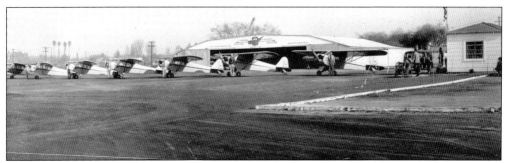

An article in the *Gazette* on January 21, 1910, read, "Attention of El Monte citizens was attracted to the buzzing noise of the propeller of an aeroplane 1,000 feet above town. Whistles were blown and people rushed out of doors and watched it go at a speed of forty miles an hour!" This photograph shows El Monte's airport in its early days.

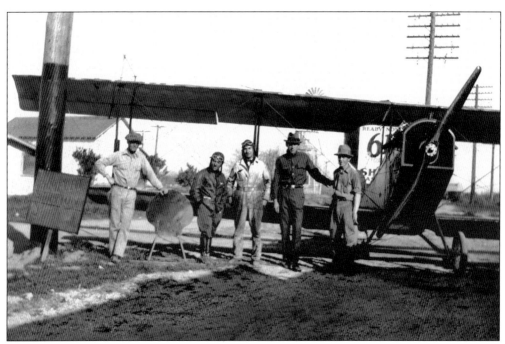

The airfield, pictured here in 1926, was west of Hoyt Avenue on the south side of Garvey Boulevard and was used for pleasure as well as for dust croppers. The airman in the middle is pilot Calley.

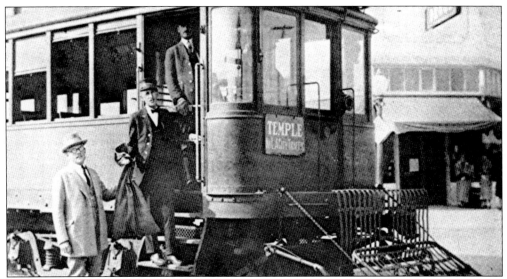

This was the first U.S. mail delivery by the Red Car at Las Tunas and Sunset Boulevard. The electric cars, called Red Cars because of their color, came through El Monte from Los Angeles in 1907. These cars were the main form of transportation for many families going to Temple City, Alhambra, or Los Angeles. The Los Angeles newspapers were sent on the last car out of town each night.

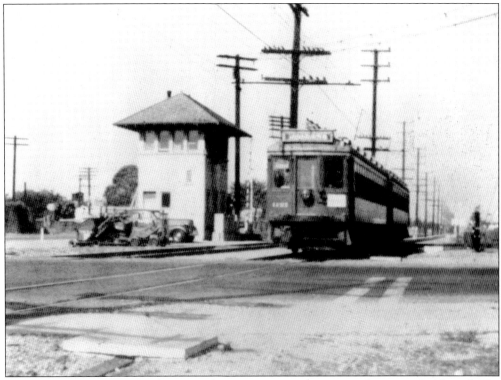

Forty years later, the Pacific Electric Red Car is at Cypress Avenue and Ramona Boulevard. The tower of the Southern Pacific Railroad, a familiar sight, is next to it. With the demise of the Red Cars, condominiums and townhouses were built in the old railroad right-of-way.

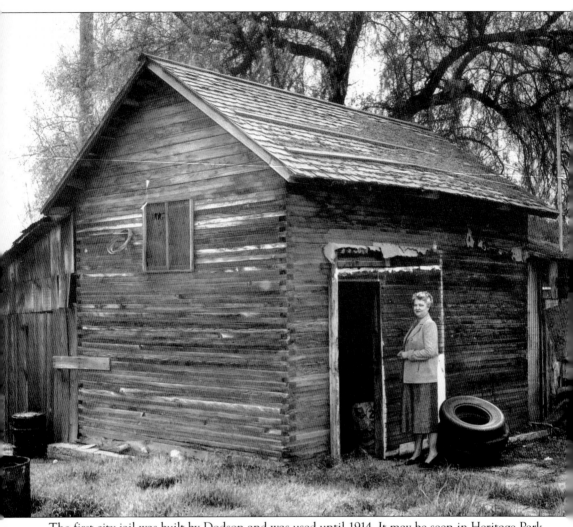
The first city jail was built by Dodson and was used until 1914. It may be seen in Heritage Park on Santa Anita Avenue in El Monte.

Two

LAW AND ORDER
MONTE BOYS STYLE

In the beginning, El Monte never experienced the lawlessness many of the wild west towns did, but it had its saloons, gambling places, shootings, horse thefts, and lynchings. It even had horse racing on Sunday along Main Street with its accompanying betting. From 1851 through 1853, there were more desperados in Los Angeles and the vicinity than in any other place on the Pacific coast. Differences were settled with knives and bullets, sheriffs and marshals were killed at pleasure, and cattle rustlers preyed upon new communities. El Monte suffered because of its close proximity to Los Angeles.

The infamous Monte Boys, a group of citizens who gained an enviable reputation for the part they played in the repression of crime in the area, were quite active during this time. Whenever an unlawful event occurred, the Monte Boys would ride into town to bring justice. Having been through the frontier experience, they were used to dealing with the rough element of human nature and were tough disciplinarians. The law was settled quickly, most often by lynching. They were most likely the inspiration for the musing of one pioneer who wrote, "There was very little law, but a large amount of good order . . . crime was rare for punishment was certain."

Today the police department is known to be both efficient and innovative. Under Chief Ken Weldon, the department received, from the State of California, the James A. Wilson Award for its community-based policy. Officers in the Reporting District Impact Program are responsible for a segment of the community. He works with these citizens on any problems they have in their neighborhood. Each citizen is given the cell phone number of the officer, who is available 24 hours a day, seven days a week. He and these people work closely to develop strong, positive relationships. Calls to the department about crimes have declined significantly in the past year. The police also work within the schools, offering programs to students about safety, drugs, and the development of friendships.

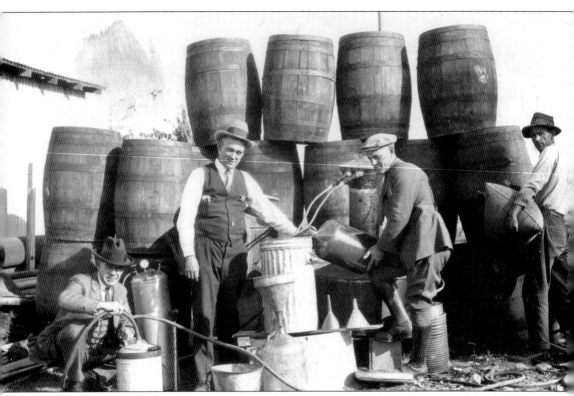

When Lester Burdick was constable, he made many trips around the country with his horse and buggy in search of desperados. Later as police chief, he cruised around in an Oldsmobile, which was the only police car available. That was alright as he was the entire police force. First chief of police Lester Burdick has confiscated some illegal liquor, which he immediately poured down the drain.

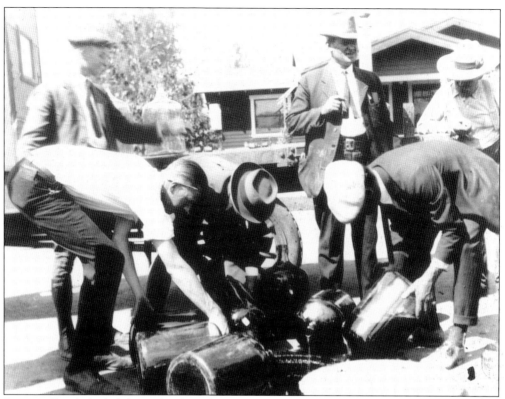

Pouring illegal alcohol down the drain kept the police busy.

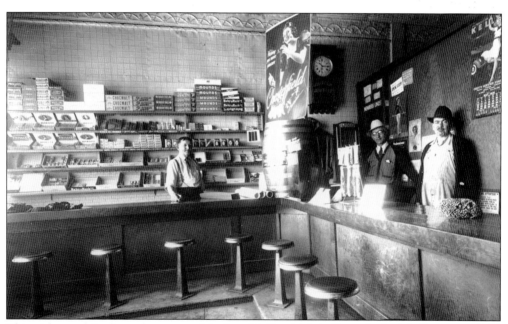

This eight-stool food stand was owned by Bert McCoy (right). He cooked while Browning (left) and chief of police Burdick (center) look on.

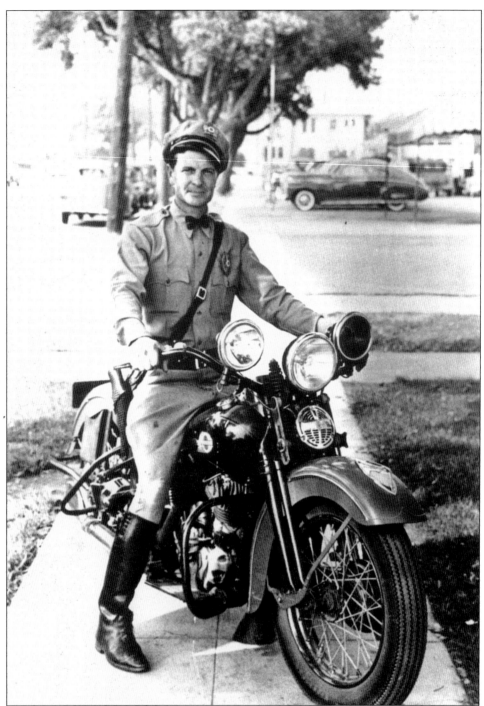

Ed Wiggins, a member of the pioneer families of Tom and Archie Wiggins, was a lifetime policeman. He was El Monte's motorcycle officer, riding an Indian motorcycle most of the time. As a motor policeman, he assisted in the capture of John Schultz, who was equipped with an armored car, and in the capture of the Southern County Bank robbers in 1936. He also served the community as chief of police.

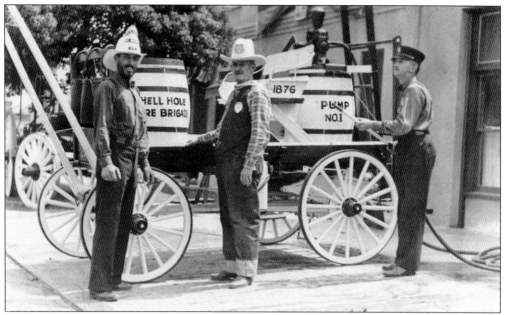

The yelling of "Fire—Fire—Fire!" or a blast from a shotgun were the alarms used by pioneers from 1870 until 1906. Water was obtained from open wells with hand pumps and windmills. On the patio of the El Monte Museum there is a nozzle, one ax, and two shovels. Here are Louis Wiggins, fire chief; Lester Burdick, chief of police; and Walter Sorenson, the one paid fireman, by the Hell Hole Fire Brigade old pump No. 1.

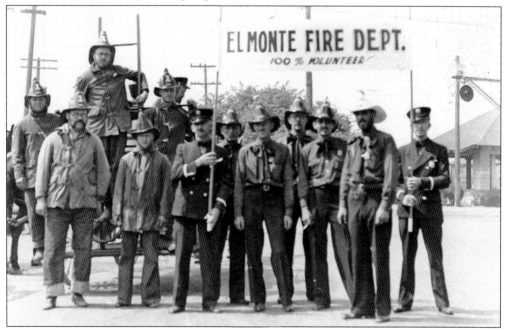

In 1914, 20 citizens agreed to form a volunteer fire department. The name chosen for this department was Hose Company No. 1. They actually had 14 volunteers. The siren on top of the water tower would sound when a fire was in progress and the volunteers would come from wherever they were in response to the alarm. Here the volunteers proudly stand in line.

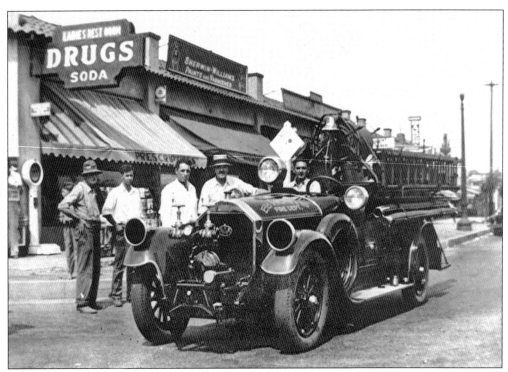

Full of pride, members of El Monte's all-volunteer fire department show off their new hook-and-ladder fire truck.

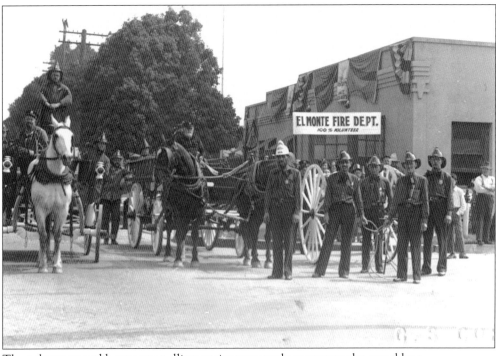

The volunteers and horses are pulling equipment, ready to put out the next blaze.

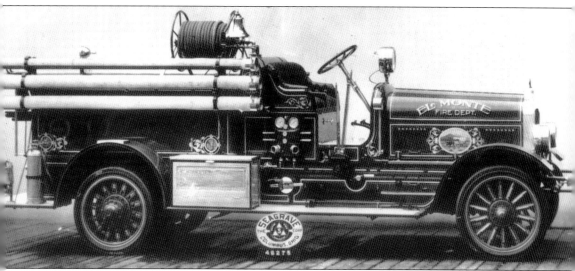

In 1922, a Ford truck was purchased and equipped with two chemical tanks, 150 feet of hose, along with approximately 500 feet of water hose. In 1926, the city purchased the Seagrave pictured here. It had a 750-gallon truck pump unit. One thousand feet of two-and-a-half-inch hose and 300 feet of one-and-one-half-inch hose were also added at this time.

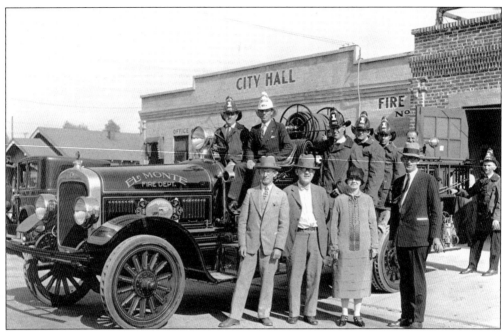

This fire station was located on Tyler Avenue next to city hall, and stalwarts of the community are standing by the shiny fire engine. In 1947, fire chief Ed Hoeft had a department of six paid employees and 10 volunteers. He began his tenure with the department in 1929.

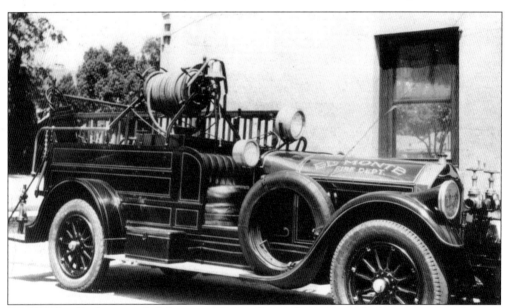

In 1931, this Ford was traded for a used Pierce Arrow limousine, which was converted into a fire truck. The chemical tanks were discarded and the 350-gallon pump was transferred to the Pierce Arrow with another 100-gallon water tank added. This, with the extra hose and the large Seagrave unit, gave the city adequate fire apparatus for practically any emergency.

Three

THE SCHOOL

To build an ideal village, it was a prime concern of both the communities of the Willows and Lexington that they build a school for the children so they could learn their letters and how to do arithmetic numbers. At that time, in 1853, milled lumber was totally out of reach and tools for building were extremely limited. However, this did not deter the citizens—their school would be built out of ingenuity.

Lining the banks of the Lexington Creek grew abundant willow groves. There were also large deposits of adobe mud along these same banks. That, along with determination, was all they needed to build the school.

The site chosen was a small shelf of sandy soil above the riverbed itself with sufficient dimensions to accommodate the structure that was planned. With this done, the school seemed to go up in no time.

The finished product was a sight to see. It was a plain structure, 20 feet by 30 feet with walls constructed of interwoven willow stems plastered with adobe mud. The roof was a simple A-frame design with the ridge and rafters made from more willow poles. The roof was covered by bundles of thatch made from the leftover cuttings in the harvested fields. A window was open on each side and an open door faced the babbling Rio Hondo River. A fire ring made from stones found along the river provided heat for the school.

This school was up and operating in 1852, hardly a year after the Thompson Party arrived. It was one of the very first public schools in the state of California.

Almost immediately, the new school began to grow . . . but not in the way one would think. Whenever rain fell, the willow stems would begin to grow. Soon the sides of the school were covered by green shoots, which had pushed their way through the adobe plaster. The villagers had to attack the willow sprouts with every knife, shears, or scissors available in Lexington and reapply new adobe to the sides. After each rain, the villagers were called not to save the school but to shave the school.

Histories of the other schools built in the community will be told through images.

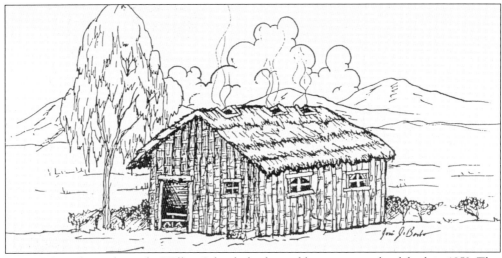

An artist's rendition shows the Willow School, the first public grammar school, built in 1852. This school was constructed on the Rio Hondo riverbank near what today is the southwest corner of Pioneer Park. Rev. J. A. Johnston, a Presbyterian minister, was Lexington's first schoolteacher. He held school every day but Sunday, and on the Sabbath, the school became the village church where Dr. Johnston would conduct a non-denominational service.

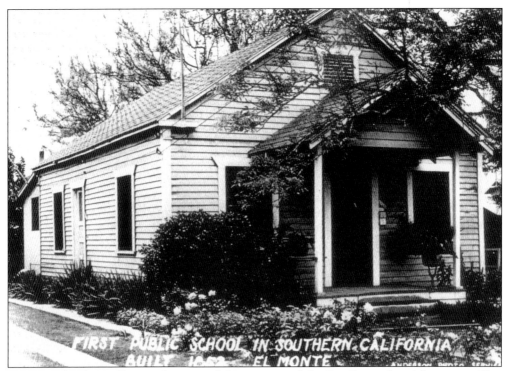

By 1853, a lumber mill opened in one of the canyons of the San Bernardino Mountains. This made it possible to build a second school building, with proper doors and shutters, to replace the Willow School. The new school was set back from the river near where the Santa Anita Fire Station is located today. The school was later used as a residence, at least through 1970.

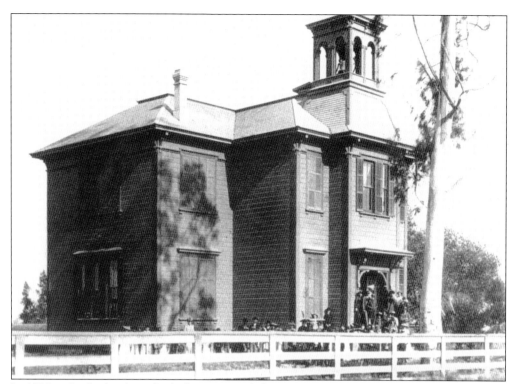

In 1880, a third school was built. It was named the Lexington Street Grammar School and was a model of late 19th-century school construction, complete with bell tower. It was a sturdy, two-story, dignified edifice that seemed to proclaim, "Let no one enter here who is not prepared to be a scholar."

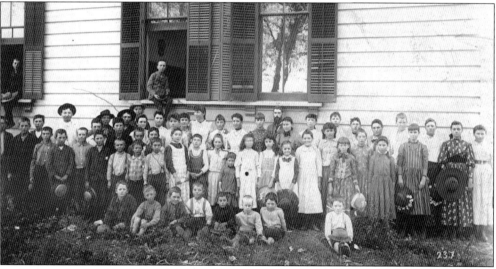

Students are by the side of the Lexington Grammar School, a building with a large and imposing exterior. From the front view, the classroom wings on either side gave a no-nonsense appearance to the entire building. Rising above all was a superb belfry containing a large bell. The bell was rung each day at the opening of school and again at its closing. That bell is now housed in front of the district office on the site of the Lexington School.

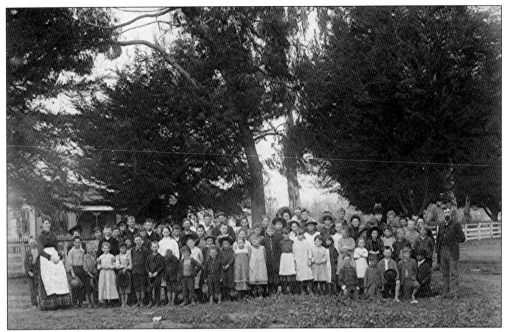

Students and teachers Miss Bowers, left, and Professor Hamilton, right, stand in the large yard behind the school. The expansive schoolyard was ringed by a triple-railed fence. Besides a play area for the children, a portion of the yard was roped off and used as pasture for the horses and mules, which many of the pupils rode to school.

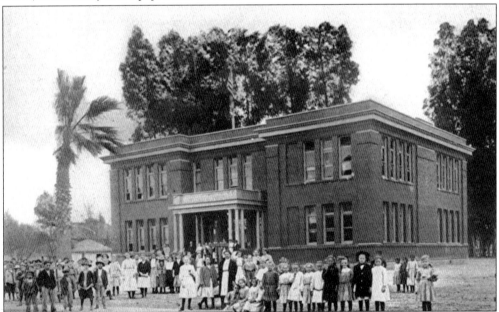

In 1909, the original Lexington Grammar School was torn down to make way for a bigger school—the Lexington School. This school was even more formidable than the one it replaced. It was a two-story, all-brick building, which housed eight classrooms and approximately 250 students. In appearance, it lacked the elegance and the architectural flair of the first Lexington School. The latter Lexington School, at best, resembled a big, red box.

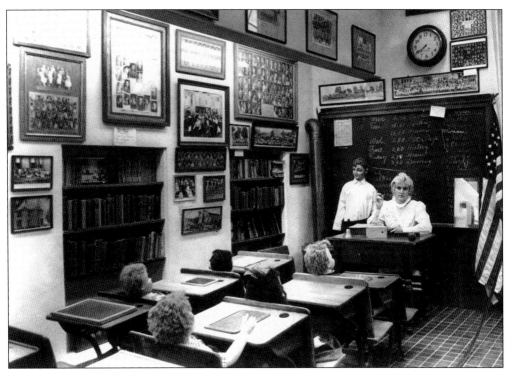
The historical museum has a school setting highlighting an original blackboard with students' names recovered during a renovation of a schoolroom and other regalia collected from the community.

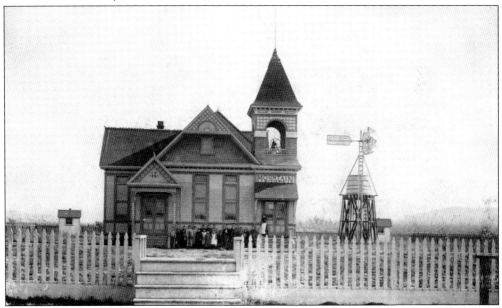
The idea for a new school to meet the needs of the children in the eastern and southern areas of El Monte was conceived and authorized in 1891 and was opened as soon as it could be built. This photograph was taken in 1897 when 20 pupils were enrolled in the one-room schoolhouse. The ubiquitous windmill water pump was in use.

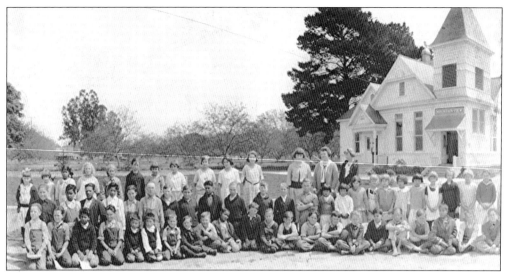
Mountain View School continued to grow and now had three teachers: Miss Haughton, Miss Edwards, and Miss Paul. In this little frame building, which boasted a belfry, the children of the pioneer grain farmers attended all elementary grades and studied the McGuffey's Reader.

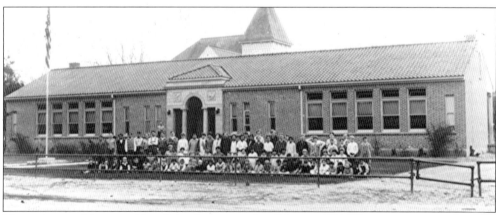
This is the new Mountain View School as pictured in February 1927. Three generations of pioneer families attended the first and/or second school. The little one-room schoolhouse is pictured rising behind the more modern building.

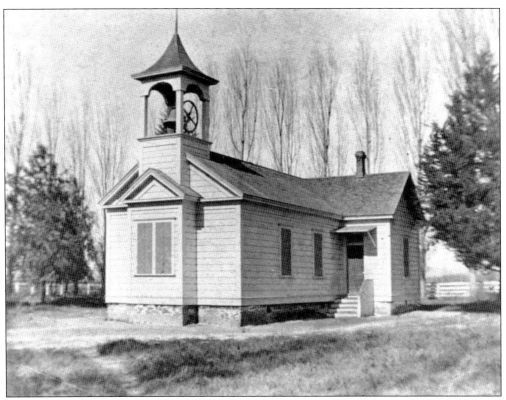

This drawing depicts the first Temple School, which was two or three miles south of old El Monte. The Temple School district, the fifth oldest in Los Angeles County, was organized March 20, 1868, under the name La Puente School District. It is now known as Valley Lindo School District.

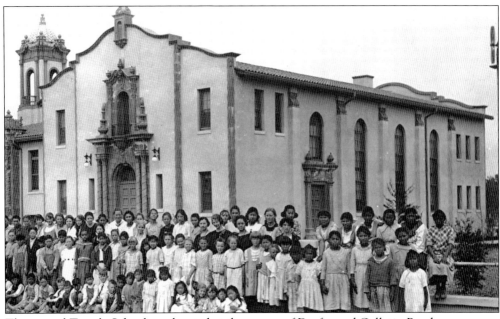

The second Temple School was located at the corner of Durfee and Gallatin Road.

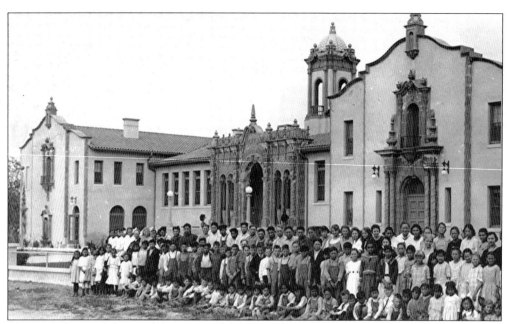
This is the front of the second Temple School.

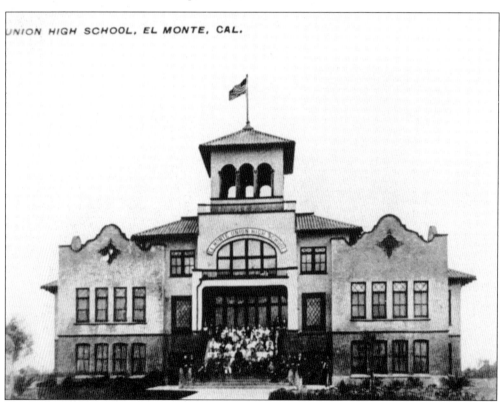
The old El Monte High School was located on the north side of Valley Boulevard, a block east of Tyler Avenue. The school had two double wings separated by a main entrance with a faux belfry and a magnificent flagstaff proudly flying Old Glory.

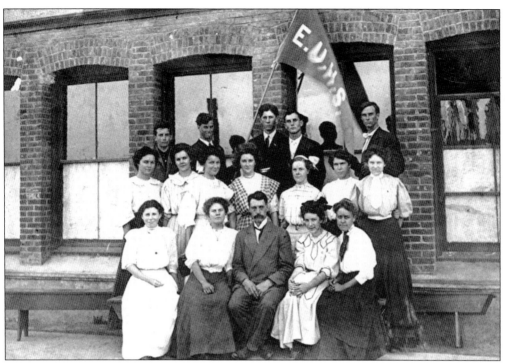
This is the El Monte High School class of 1906, the first year the new school was operating.

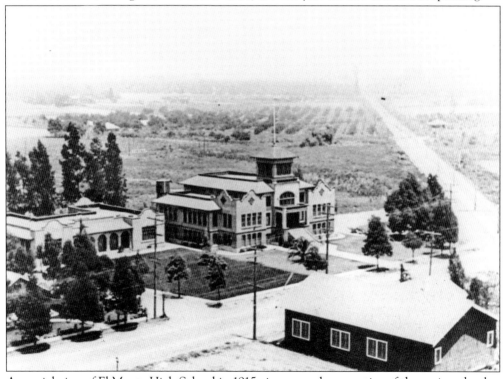
An aerial view of El Monte High School in 1915 gives a good perspective of the entire school at that date. The school faced Main Street (Valley Boulevard) with Tyler Avenue to its east.

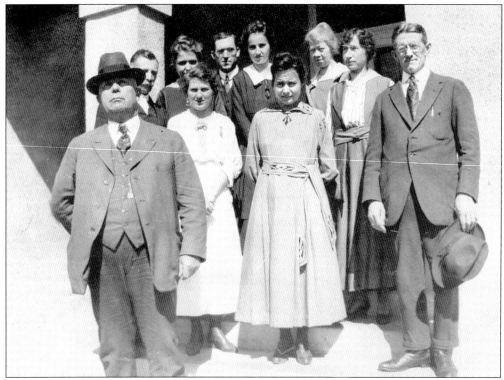

The El Monte High School faculty in 1919–1920 includes Mr. Babcock, principal, at far left. Some of the teachers are Lloyd Wright, math; Viola Marshall, home economics; Mildred Davidson, Spanish and English; Sal Meierk, commercial; William Simpson, woodwork and shop; and Gertrude Uhl, English.

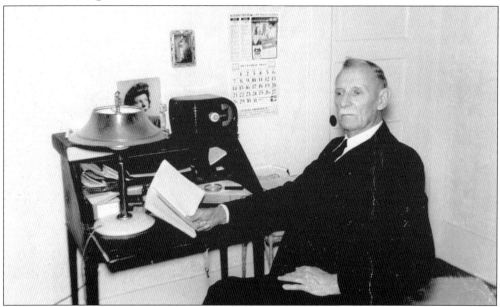

Lloyd Wright was a revered math teacher at El Monte High School for many years. His son was Frank M. Wright, for whom one of the El Monte Elementary schools was named.

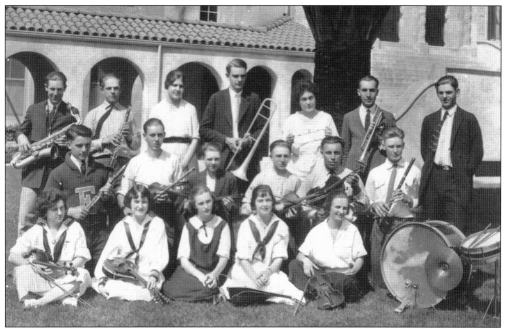

The El Monte High School orchestra is in front of the old high school in the early 1900s. Note the Mission-style architecture of the school.

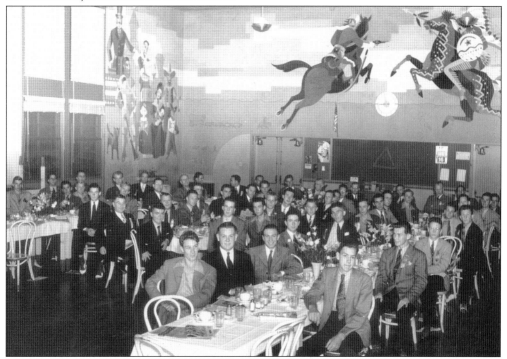

The new high school, built in 1939, had many murals painted by the Work Progress Administration (WPA) artists. The WPA was created to provide economic relief to the citizens of the United States who were affected by the Great Depression. This photograph shows some of the murals in the cafeteria. Unfortunately these paintings were not saved during necessary renovation of the school.

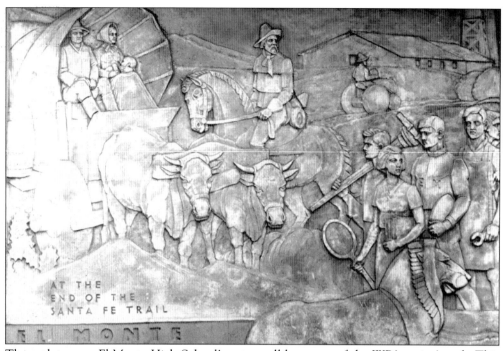

The sculpture on El Monte High School's outer wall has more of the WPA artists' work. This depicts the end of Santa Fe Trail.

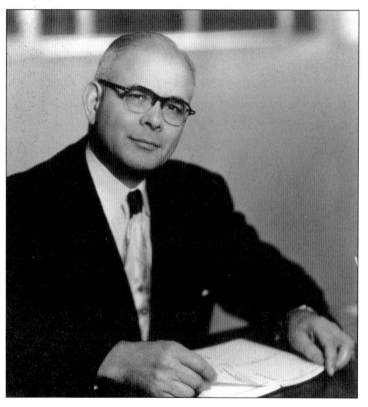

Robert S. Hicks was superintendent of El Monte High School from 1936 to 1952. His philosophy was to give the youth the appropriate educational program that would help them do the things they would be doing as adults much better. He instituted industrial and graphic arts, music, home economics, art, health, family living, and social living into the curriculum at EMHS.

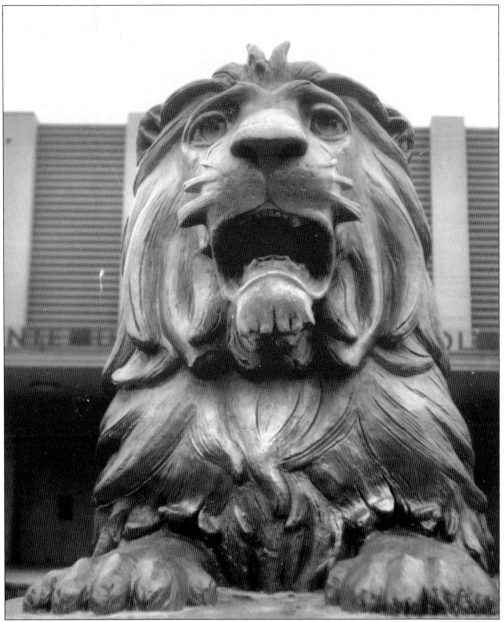

A lion guards the portals of El Monte High School. As Jack Barton, principal, wrote in the frontispiece of the Lions' 1982 yearbook:

> The Lion; Kingly Patron of our School,
> The Symbol of our Pride and Courage,
> A Monument of historical significance to our community,
> The Lion; A Silent Sentry at the portals of our Alma Mater,
> But his Roar echoes in the hearts of all of us.

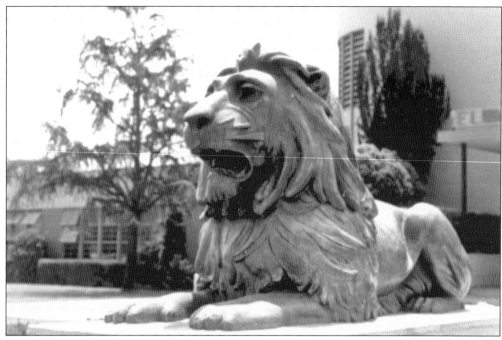

Donated by Mr. Gay, the original statue stands at the entrance to the school. Its golden patina is an example of the adoration and care the generations of students have shown to their roaring mascot.

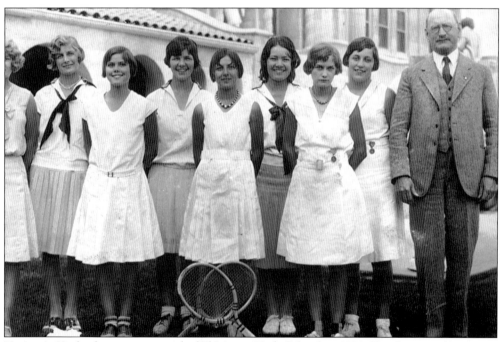

Henry A. Keeley became principal of El Monte High School in 1920. He also served as tennis coach for the school. He is seen here with the 1929–1930 girls tennis team. Pictured, from left to right, are Betty Cleminson, Margaret Irwin, Jean Bunning, Bonnie Jean Potter, Nadine Coates, Lois Choens, Phyllis Young, Ruth Darling, and Mr. Keeley.

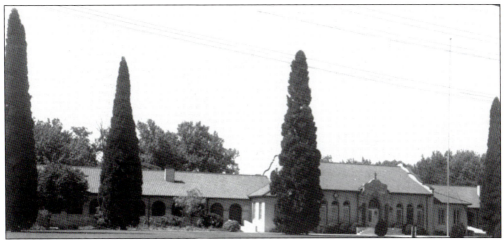

On September 8, 1922, the school board of trustees purchased 13 acres on Columbia Street to build a new grammar school. In 1923, Columbia Grammar School was constructed with 10 rooms to house the students.

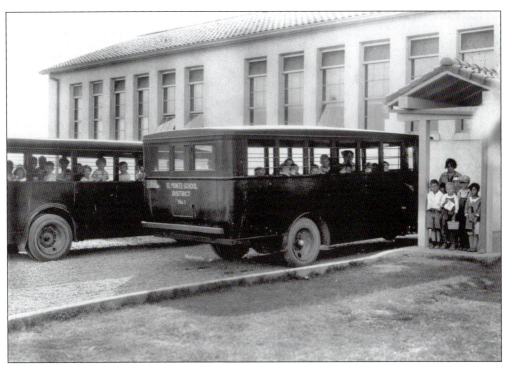

These were the first school buses for Columbia Grammar School. Note the covered waiting area built to keep the rain off the students.

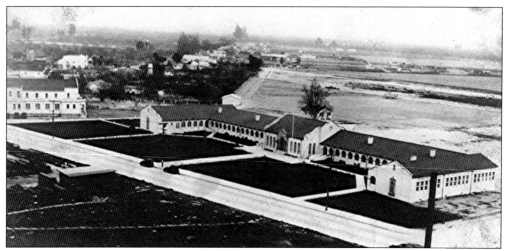

This 1924 aerial view shows the red-tile roof of the Columbia Grammar School. This school also follows Mission-style architecture. To the left of the school is the Presbyterian church on Valley Boulevard and Columbia Street.

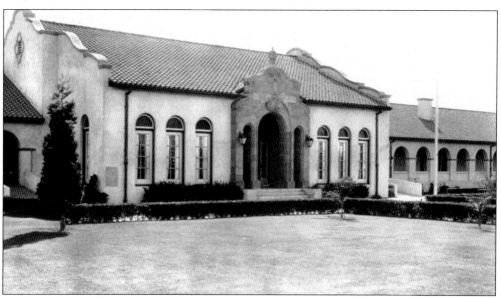

This photograph from the 1920s or 1930s shows the front of Columbia School and the tiled roof. Although the school went through many changes and growth throughout the years, the last of the red tiles were not removed until the 1980s.

Four

THE LION FARM
A ROARING SUCCESS

The arrival in 1923 of the famous Gay's Lion Farm brought El Monte an outstanding tourist attraction. For the next 20 years, people came from everywhere to see this one and only lion exhibit. Gay's Lion Farm has been likened to the Disneyland of the 1920s and 1930s.

Mr. and Mrs. Charles Gay, European by birth, came to Southern California in the early 1920s with the idea of raising wild animals for use in the burgeoning motion-picture industry. Their dream came true with the establishment of the lion farm in El Monte, locating here because of the availability of suitable acreage and the relative proximity to the film centers of Los Angeles.

At its peak, the farm housed over 200 African lions. The site consisting of a U-shaped compound with separate individual cages for the adult lions, a larger nursery cage for the expected population of playful cubs, and a very large, centrally located arena cage where the trained lions, under the whip and gun of Gay, performed a spectacular wild animal act for the massed spectators. Many of the lions did star in numerous motion pictures during the 1920s and 1930s.

A very strong affinity developed between El Monte and its feline citizens. The affection was best represented when, in 1925, the teams from El Monte High School eagerly took on the nickname of the "Lions." Gay responded to this gesture by periodically designating one of the young, active male lions as the official mascot of the school. It followed naturally that the mascot would make its appearance at certain home football games, and the crowds of cheering supporters were supplemented by the full-throated rumbling roar of their patron beast.

World War II saw the demise of the lion farm. With the strict rationing of horse meat and gasoline, the establishment closed its doors for the duration, and the lions were farmed out to public zoos throughout the country. Today the only reminder of the farm is the magnificent statue that now stands gleaming golden in the sunlight in its eternal vigilance at the portals of El Monte's Lion campus.

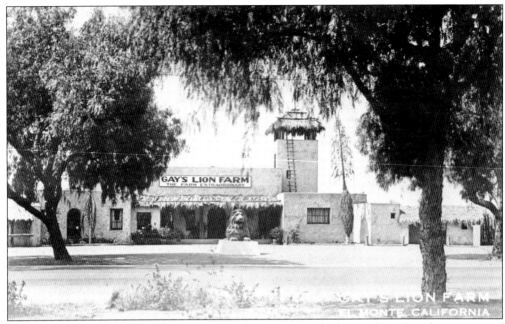

Gay's Lion Farm, situated in El Monte a short distance from the heart of Los Angeles, was one of the outstanding tourist attractions in Southern California. To visit the great southwest and not see this lion farm was akin to going to Egypt and not seeing the pyramids. This is the entrance to the lion farm, which was the only one of this kind in the world at that time. It existed from 1925 until 1942. A statue of Leo sits in the entranceway guarding all that lies within

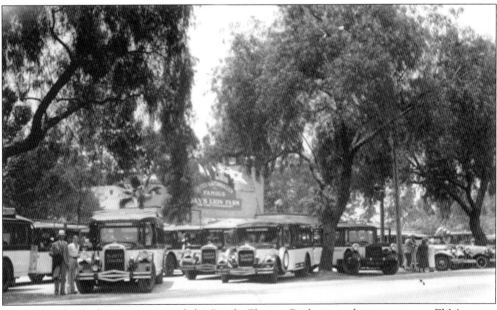

On weekends, the bus company and the Pacific Electric Railway made extra runs to El Monte to accommodate the many visitors. Excursion buses are pictured in a lot surrounded by pepper trees.

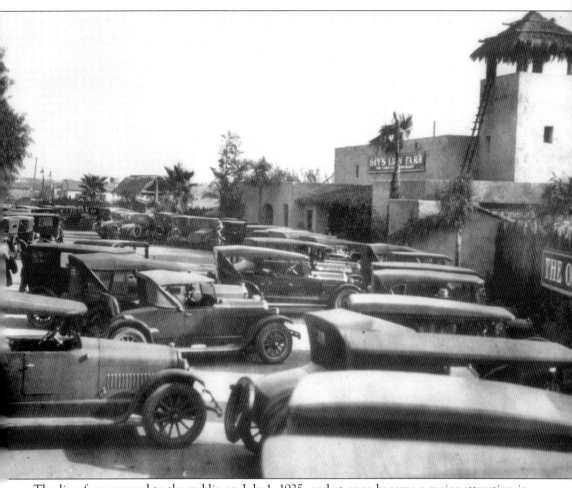

The lion farm opened to the public on July 1, 1925, and at once became a major attraction in Southern California. Visitors flocked here from all over the southland: by car, bus, and the Pacific Electric Red Car

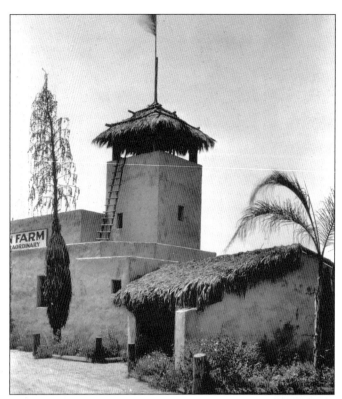

A jungle theme was maintained throughout the farm so the illusion that visitors were in the jungles of darkest Africa was everywhere.

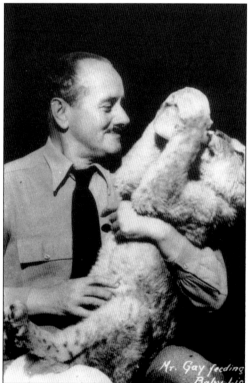

Charles Gay is feeding a baby lion from the nursery, which housed the most recent generation of cubs produced at the farm.

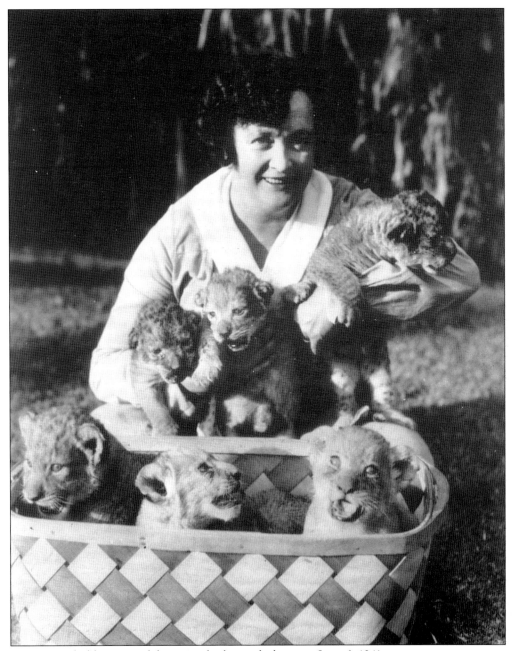
Mrs. Gay is holding two of the sextuplet lion cubs born on June 6, 1941.

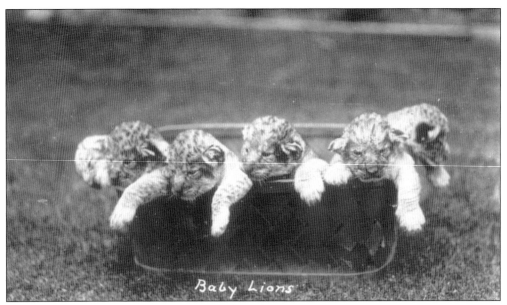

The six little babies in the tub have not yet lost their spots.

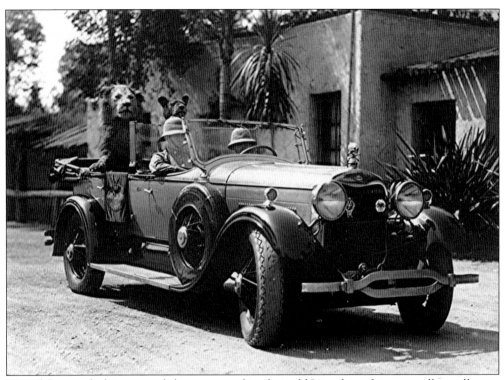

Two of the guards drive around the compound in their old Lincoln making sure all is well.

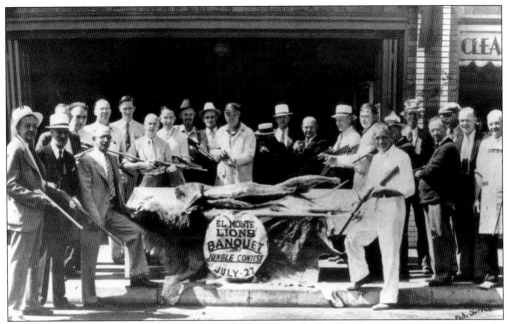

Each year, the El Monte Lions Club hosted a banquet, which served some lion but mostly pork, chicken, or beef. This banquet was held July 27, 1934. Those pictured here include Roy Addleman, Reverend Putman, Lee Writer, Ken Anderson, Fred King, Frank Wright, Del Steers, Sam Leffler, Lester Burdick, Hal Westfall, Bob Helman, Jim Nixon, and Harold Pearson.

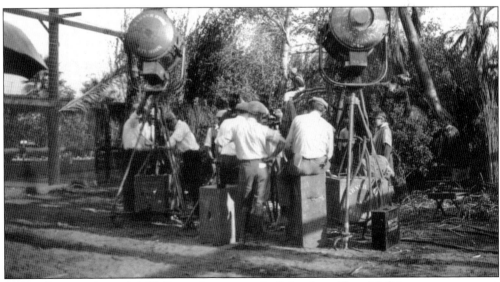

Lights, Camera, Action! A Hollywood crew sets the lights for a film with lions.

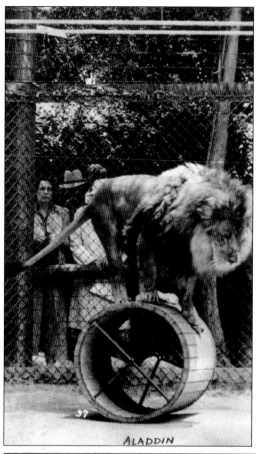

Spectators watch Aladdin roll the wheel.

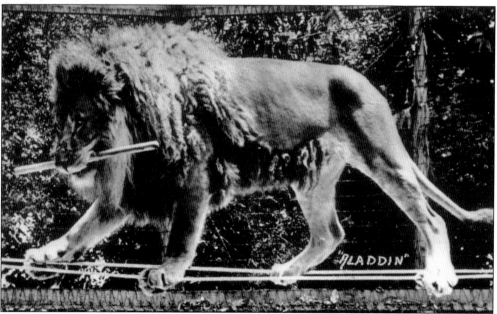

Here the versatile Aladdin walks a tightrope holding a stick in his mouth.

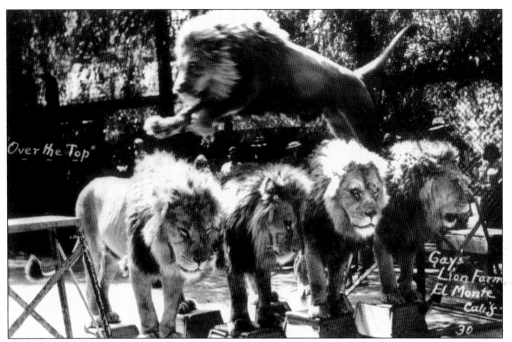

Is this a giant leap or could one say a lion leap?

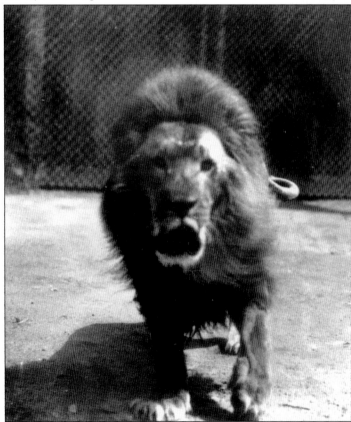

How would you like to meet this beast in the jungle?

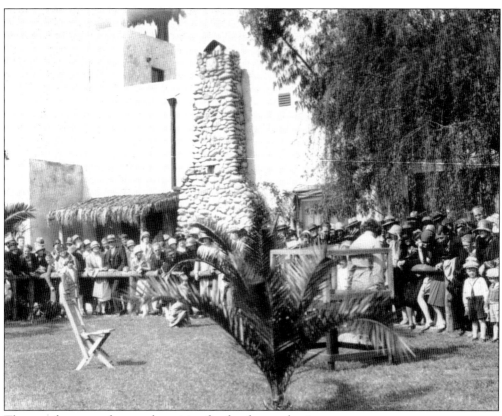
The crowd seems to be eagerly waiting for the show to begin.

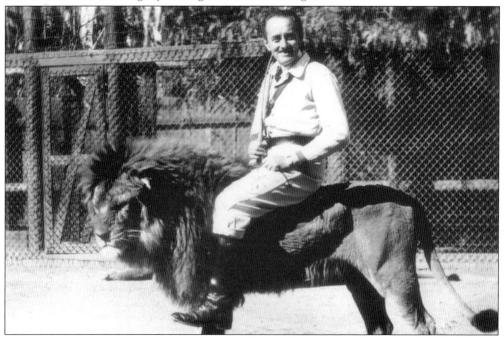
Charles Gay looks happier than the lion that is taking him for a ride.

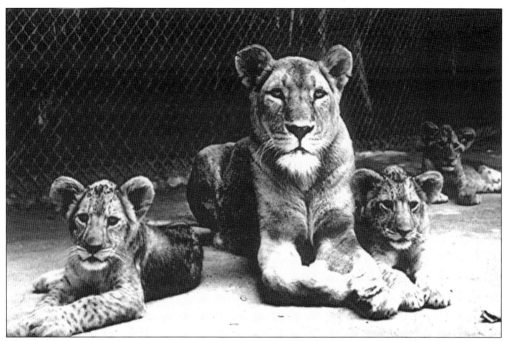
This family appears to be content sunning themselves and looking at visitors joyfully staring back.

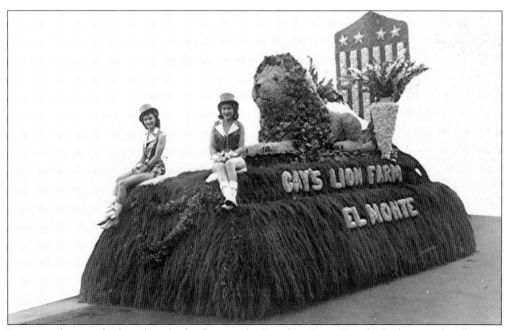
For several years, the lion farm had a float in the Pasadena Rose Parade. Riding on this float are two high school students, Marian King on the left and Marjorie Kneedler on the right.

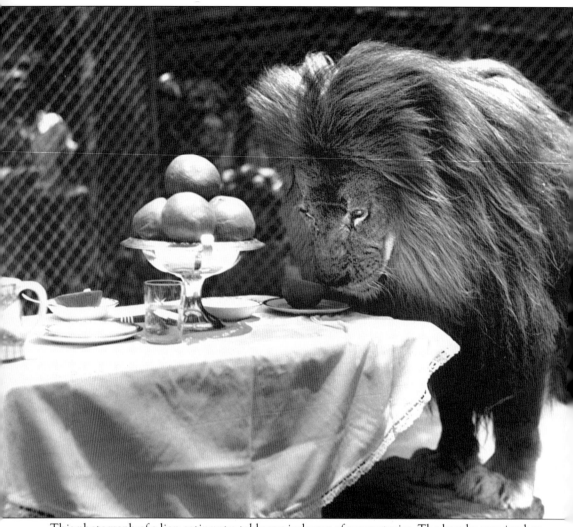

This photograph of a lion eating at a table reminds one of many stories. The best known is when the lion mascot Peter was invited to the football banquet. Peter would try to echo the players in song and cheers by emitting throaty growls, but, as the cheering increased, he became imbued with the spirit of the evening and gave forth several real lion roars. In the meantime, the PTA ladies were serving plates of roast turkey, and as they passed through the swinging doors, they had to pass Peter. As the odor of the turkey excited him, he would thrust his paw through the iron bars and try to get some of the feast. It is not known how successful he was, but he certainly frightened the PTA servers.

Five
EL MONTE IN THE 20TH CENTURY

Memories—the village, the farms, the willows, and reeds—are all gone. Even the flowing water that enticed the pioneers to this land is now harnessed through cement channels on its way to the sea.

Population increased steadily in the early 1930s, and with more people, continuous improvements were made. New homes were built, schools to accommodate the children were added, utility services had to be updated, the business district grew, and many other needed changes came about.

Beginning in 1935, the early days of this community were honored with yearly pioneer celebrations consisting of parades, pageants, rodeos, barbeques, horse races, and dancing in the street. A spectacular horse and horse-drawn vehicle parade, which included approximately 1,000 horses, was several miles long. Every woman and girl in town dressed in costumes, while the male population wore bandanas, guns, holsters, and boots. If a man was caught without a beard or other facial hair, he was publicly dunked in a tub of water. Ending the three-day celebration, religious services were held in various churches. In 1936, city clerk Ruth Bruton was named Queen of Pioneer Days. That year, a professional rodeo was attended by 8,000 persons, while about 40,000 watched the long and colorful parade.

After the start of World War II, there was a decline in celebration, and at the present, Pioneer Days is celebrated by the descendents of those early day pioneers with a picnic every summer. During World War II, all attention turned to the patriotic activities taking place throughout the country. Ration books were distributed, war bonds purchased, and Red Cross participation more than tripled. Young men anxiously awaited the announcement of their army draft numbers or they volunteered for other branches of the military. Many women joined the WAACS or nursing field to tend to injured soldiers.

All citizens of El Monte, as well as of the nation, eagerly waited for the end of the war and the return of the young people.

After the war, when the men and women returned home to their loved ones, El Monte mushroomed and once again was busy with the building of new homes, businesses, and schools.

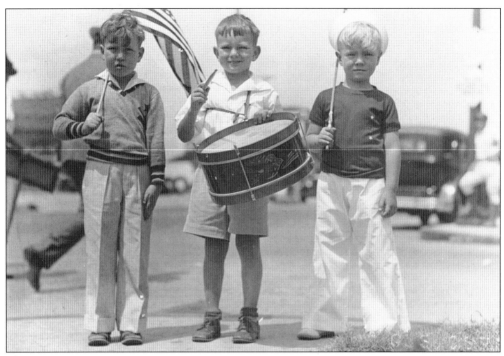
As with people from cities all over the country, El Monte loved parades. This Memorial Day parade in 1932 features three little charmers—Alex McKay, Billy Haughton, and Edsel Corpe.

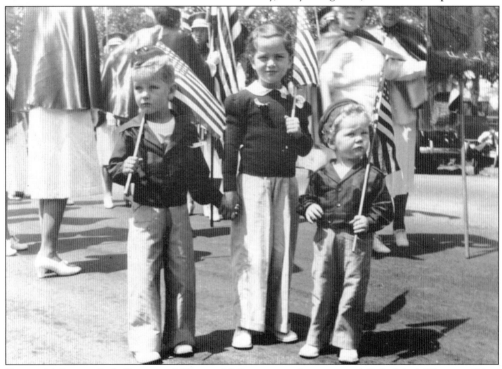
Denny McIntyre, Judy Freer, and Timmy McIntyre are three more delightful children walking down the street.

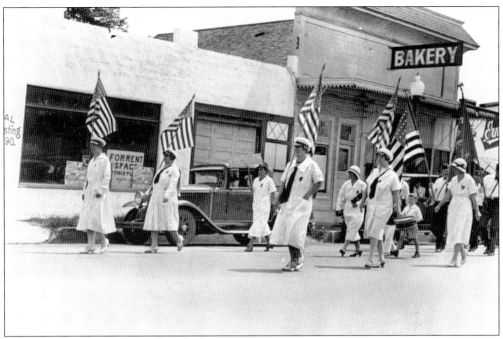

These patriotic women in white are marching down Valley Boulevard in the same parade.

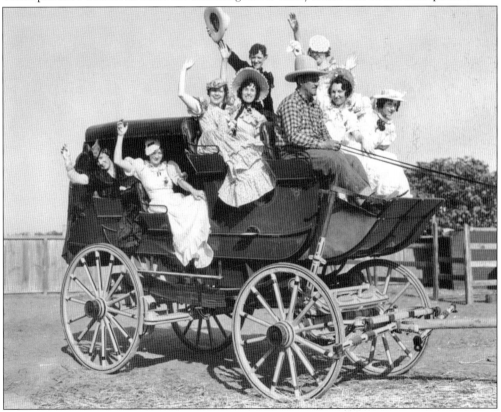

In the 1930s, stagecoaches played a major role in the Pioneer Day parades.

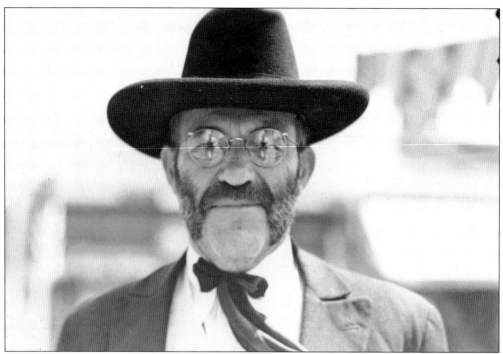

Ephram Shirpser is a son of Soloman Shirpser who came to California from Poland in 1860. Here, in May 1936, he is ready for Pioneer Days. If the men did not have hair growing somewhere on their head, they were publicly dunked in a barrel of water and usually fined.

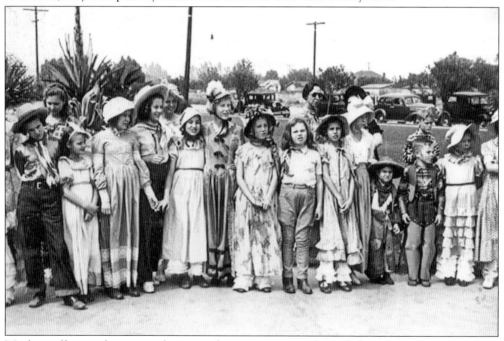

Mothers all over the city and surrounding community showed their ingenuity in making costumes for their girls and themselves. These are school children showing off their new dresses and bonnets.

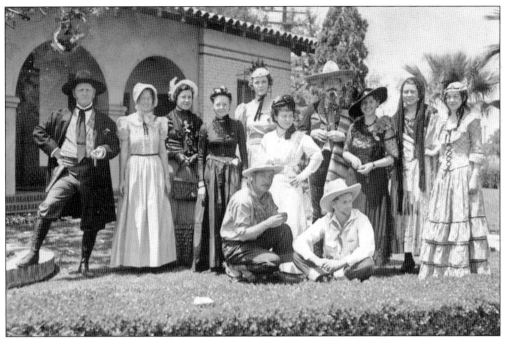

This image of Pioneer Days includes both pioneer and Spanish representations.

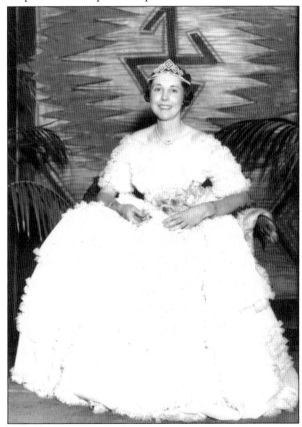

Ruth Bruton was crowned queen of the first Pioneer Days in 1935. She was also city clerk at the time.

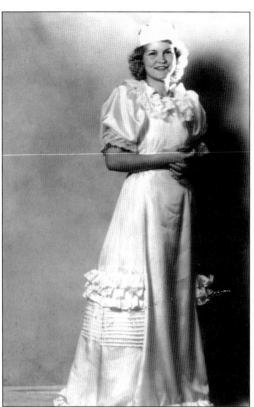

The following year, Dorothy Redd was crowned queen by California governor Frank Merriam.

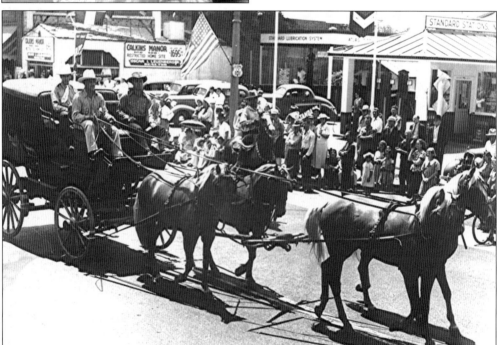

Bob Phoell and his matched team of Palominos led a stagecoach in the 1936 parade. Here they are at the intersection of Main Street and Tyler Avenue.

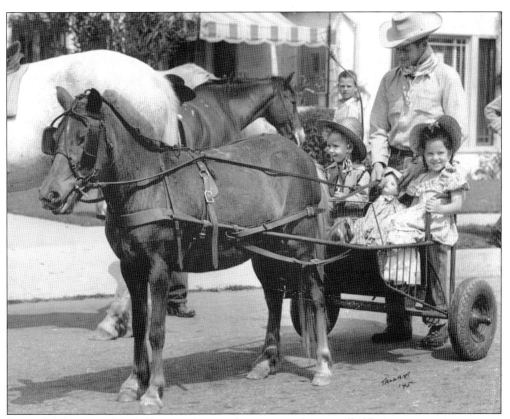

Denny McIntyre and Judy Freer are having fun in a cart being pulled by a pony.

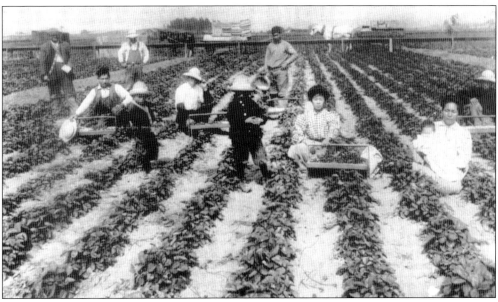

The Nagai family is pictured on their farm in 1914. They continued to farm and grow the freshest produce in town until the advent of World War II when the Japanese were interred in a more central part of the United States.

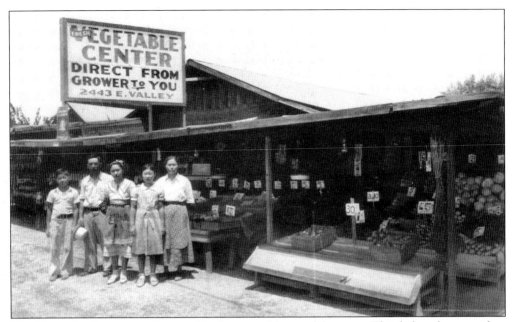

The Nagai family grew produce and had a vegetable stand for years. This led to the store they owned on Lower Azusa Avenue.

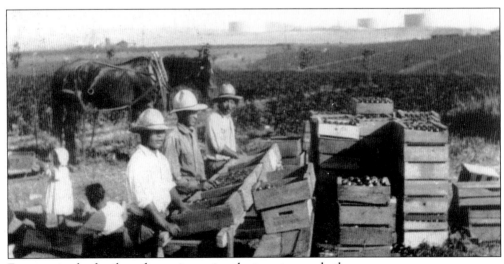

Everyone in the family took part in crating the tomatoes and other crops.

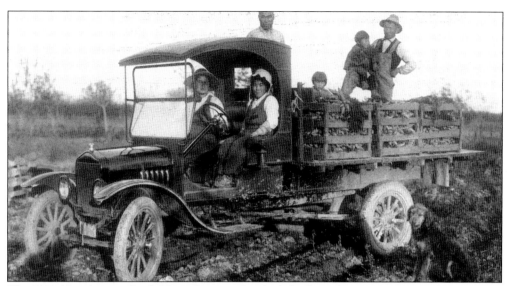
The entire family is in the fields in their truck, which leads to the expression "truck farming."

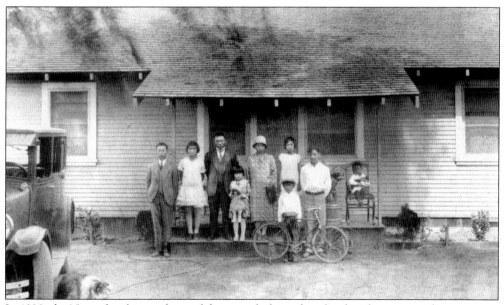
In 1930, the Nagai family is in front of their porch dressed up for church or some other occasion.

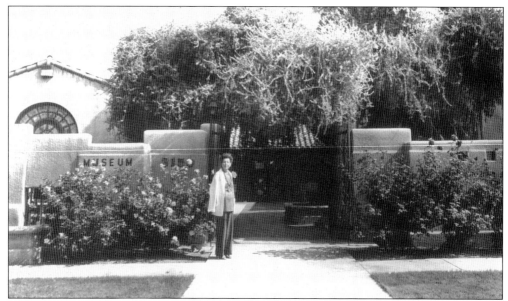

Lillian Wiggins, former curator of the museum from 1960 to 1980, is standing in front of the museum. Married into a pioneer family, she collected much old furniture and clothing from others, which is on display in the museum. The current curator is Donna Crippen, another person who, along with her late husband, has been extremely active in civic affairs.

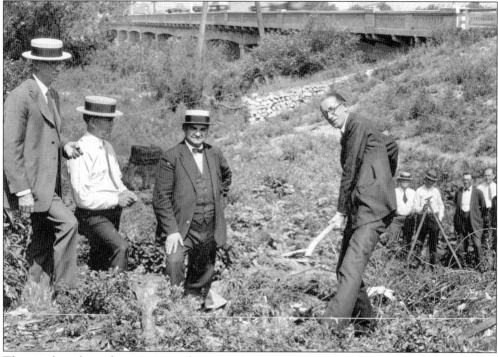

The city has always been interested in providing supervised swimming for the children of El Monte. The first community plunge was built in 1925. This photograph shows the groundbreaking ceremony for the first of three pools, with Goodspeed Corpe, Judge Ranger, Ephraim Shirpser, Lester Burdick, and others civic leaders digging in.

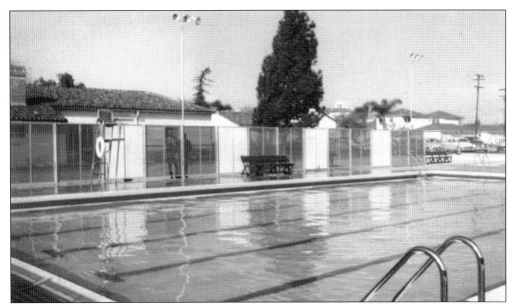

The second pool in town, built behind the community center and across the street from the high school, had dual purposes—the public could use it after school and on the weekends and the high school could conduct swimming classes during the day.

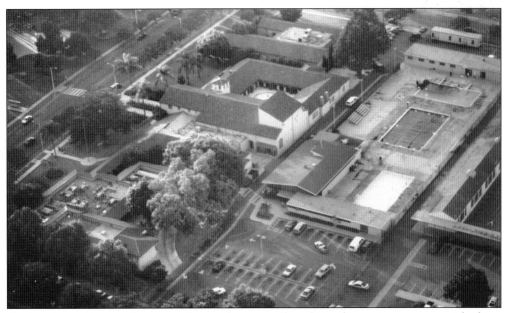

At the time, this was the most advanced system of pools in the entire country, with three graduated pools—one for waders, another for junior swimmers, and one for accomplished divers and swimmers.

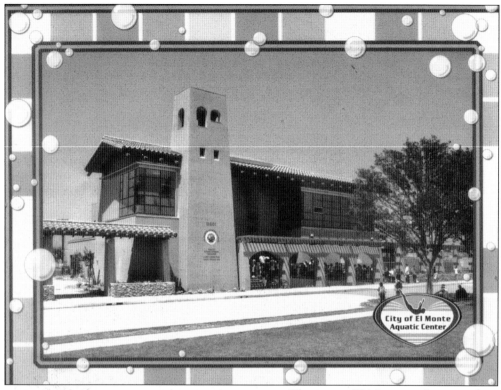

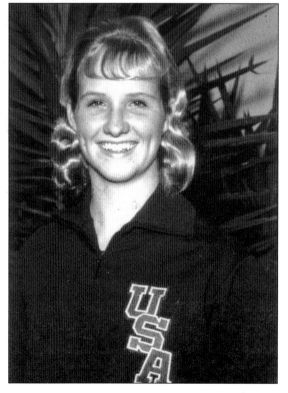

The newest El Monte pool is more than a pool, it is an aquatic center built in honor of Sandy Neilson and Lance Larson, two El Monte High School graduates who were Olympic medalists. It is located just north of the second pool across from the El Monte Museum, adjacent to Tyler Avenue.

Sandy Neilson won three gold medals in 1972 at the Olympic Games in Munich. Wearing the USA uniform, she won medals for the 100-meter freestyle, the 400-meter freestyle relay, and the 400-meter medley relay.

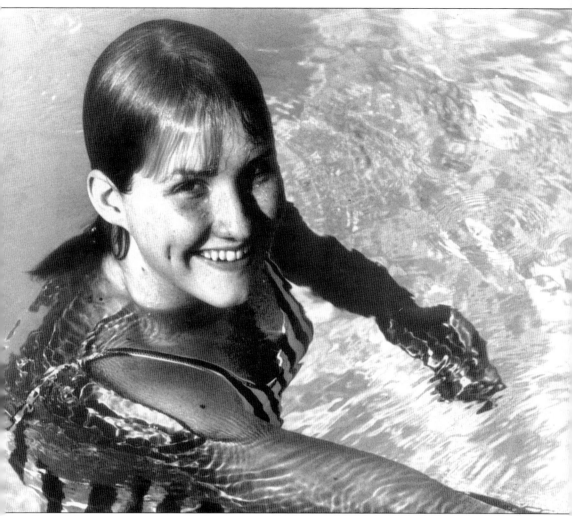
Sandy Neilson is enjoying a refreshing swim at the El Monte pool. In 1986, she was inducted into the International Swimming Hall of Fame, and in 2005, as Sandy Neilson-Bell, she was inducted into the Masters Swimming Hall of Fame. She accumulated 43 Masters' world records for freestyle, individual medley, and sprint butterfly. She also is in the El Monte High School Hall of Fame.

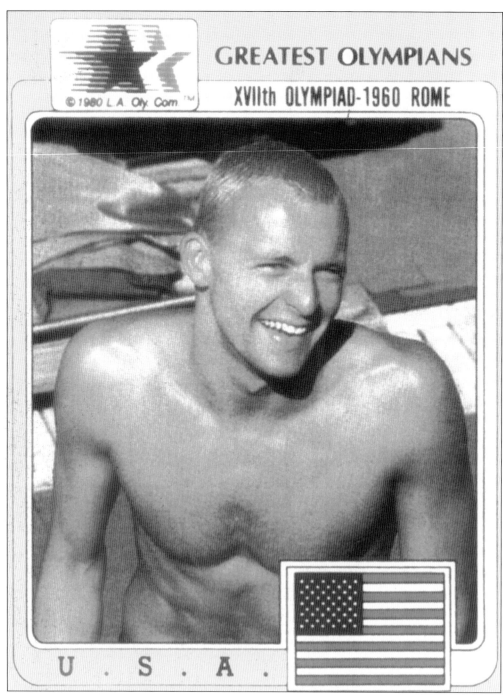

Lance Larson won an Olympic gold and silver medal at the 1960 games in Rome. He was inducted into the International Swimming Hall of Fame as an Honor Swimmer in 1980. He won his Olympic gold medal on the butterfly leg of the 400-meter medley relay with a split time of 58 seconds but is best known for the controversy over his dead heat, 100-meter freestyle silver medal in the same games.

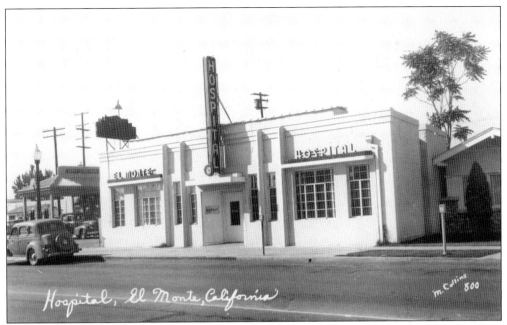

El Monte Hospital was the main alternative to Los Angeles General Hospital from the 1920s until after World War II and was run by Dr. Stanley. It was located on the corner of Main Street and Tyler Avenue.

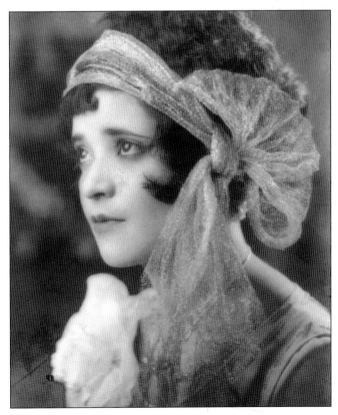

Frances "Quica" Ortiz was a resident of Medina Court in the 1920s.

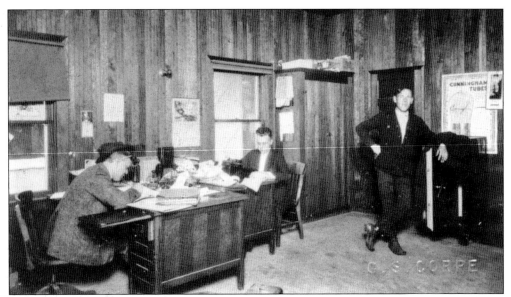
In early 1923, the Coast Radio Station was founded by Goodspeed Corpe, an amateur radio operator in El Monte.

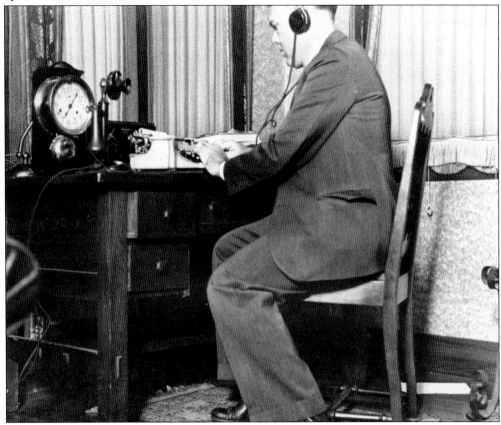
A radio operator is transmitting from KUY, an El Monte station that could be heard as far as Seattle, Washington. It was considered quite a feat in the early 1920s.

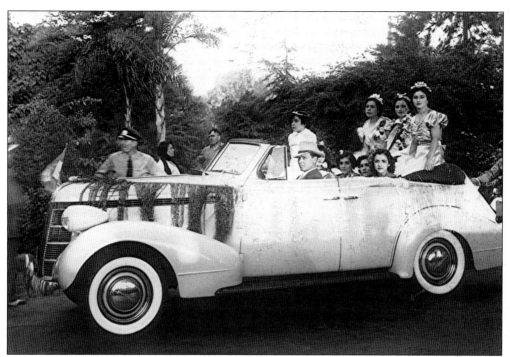
Mexican Independence Day was celebrated at Medina Court on September 16, 1930. The royal court is in the car with the queen sitting in the middle of the back seat and the little girl, Tona Ortiz, seated in the front.

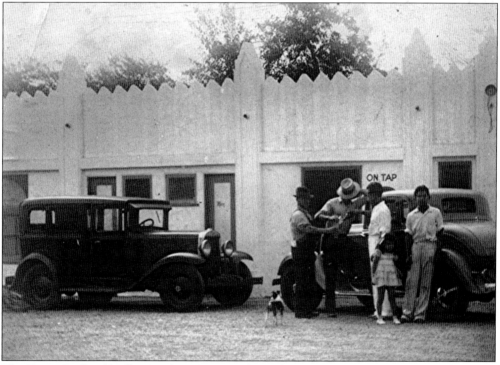
The Tango Bar/Pool Hall in Medina Court in the mid-1930s was owned by Tony Ortiz.

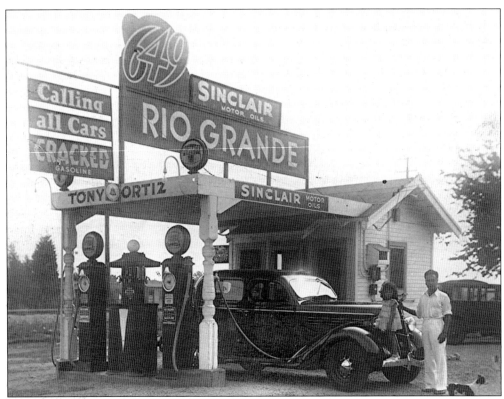

This is the Rio Grande Gas Station on Peck Road at Medina Court during the 1930s.

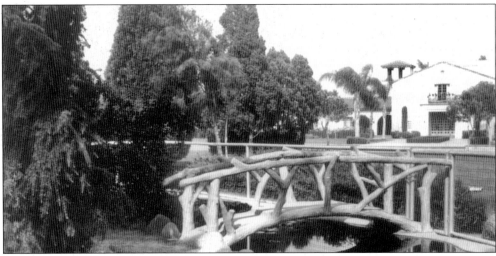

The koi pond and bridge in the El Monte Community Park delighted children in the 1930s when the park was first built. In 1946, it was renamed the El Monte Memorial Park in honor of the veterans who fought for this country. Later the name was changed to the Tony Acero Park in memory of an El Monte policeman who was killed when he became involved in a robbery in a neighboring town while off duty.

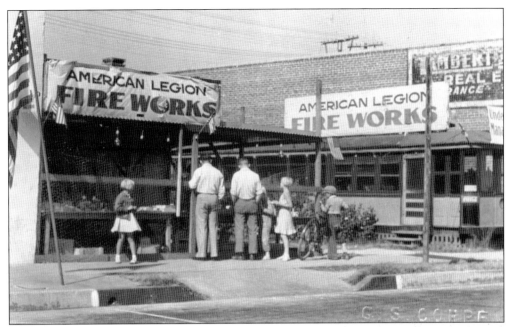

In the 1930s, it was legal to sell fireworks to the public. This is one of the many American Legion stands operating in those days, a moneymaker for them.

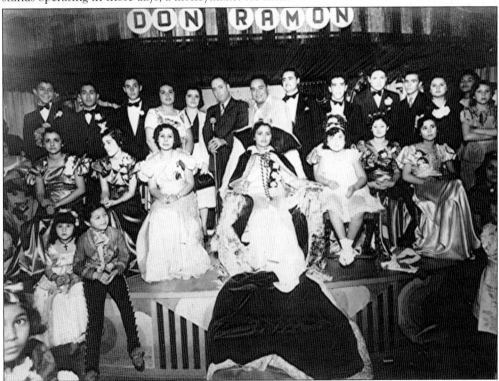

The new Swanee River on Valley Boulevard was the location for a New Year's Eve party on December 31, 1937. They are having a swinging good time. This building was a dance hall and nightclub owned by Tony Ortiz.

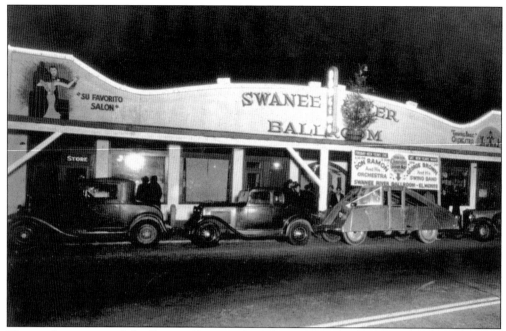

This is the exterior of the Swanee River nightclub. In the early days of El Monte, there was another Swanee River nightclub, but it burned down.

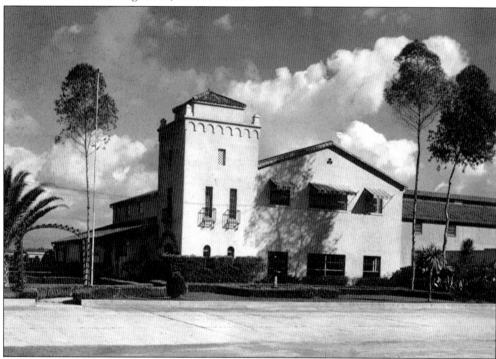

The flower fields of the Bodger Seed Company were moved long ago to Lompoc, California, but the warehouse, seen here, is still located at the same spot it has been for years—at Tyler Avenue and Thienes Road in El Monte. Third- and fourth-generation Bodgers are now running the business.

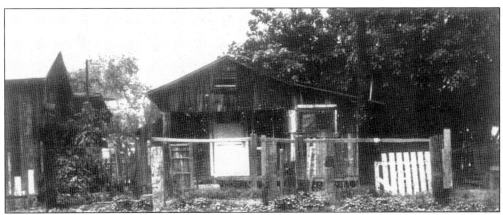
Samuel Hicks built homes near the railroad for the men who worked there. The families could rent these houses from him cheaply. It stands to reason that it became known as Hick's Camp.

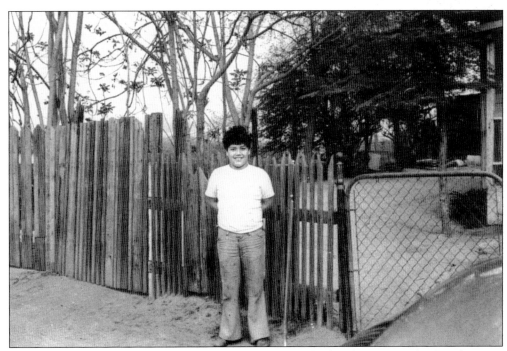
The children from Hick's Camp attended Lexington and Columbia elementary schools. When new schools were built, they attended Gidley and Shirpser Schools, named for two early pioneers.

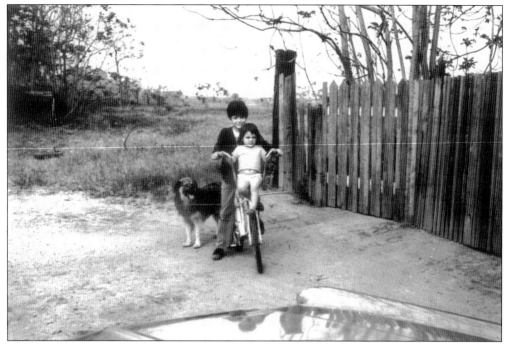

Two children go for a ride at Hick's Camp.

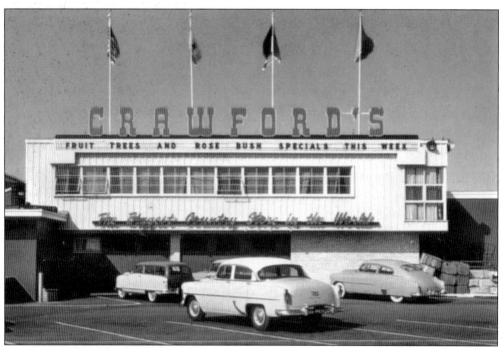

At Crawford's giant shopping center in Five Points, El Monte, the flags and the huge sign on the marquee were a familiar landmark to residents and tourists nearing Los Angeles from the desert area. Crawford's was famous all over America as the largest country store in the world, and each week, over 70,000 people shopped under its giant roof for everything from apples to airplanes.

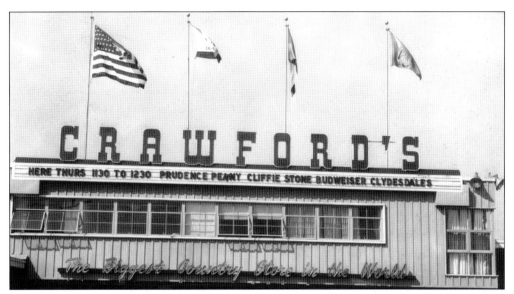

This is another photograph of Crawford's, the biggest country store in the world. Note the appearances on Thursday from 11:30 a.m. to 12:30 p.m. being Prudence Penny, Cliffie Stone, and the Budweiser Clysdales. It was quite a lineup for an hour show in little El Monte.

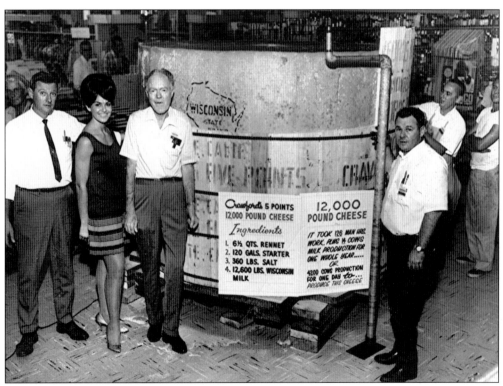

Known as the biggest little country store in the world, Crawford's always went for big things. Here is pictured the Big Cheese, 12,000 pounds of cheese, an attraction meant to increase sales.

111

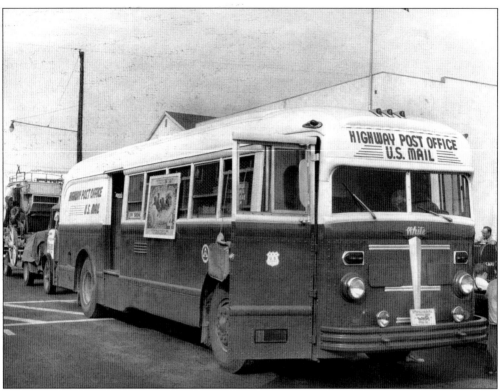

Before the United States Postal Service moved mail via air, they used highway mail buses, as seen here. Besides these buses, trains, the Red Car, and ships were also used to transport the mail.

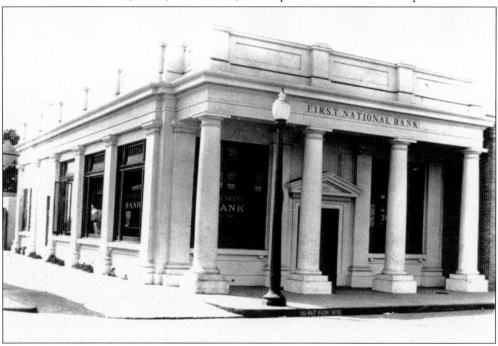

The First National Bank was built in 1935 on the corner of Palm Court and Main Street.

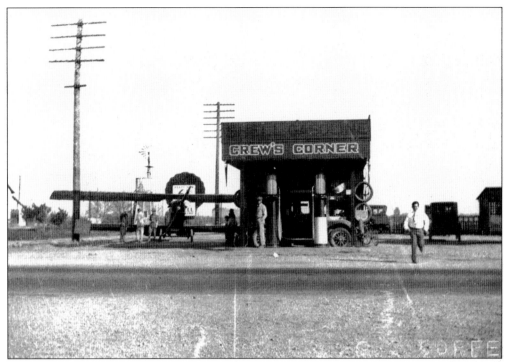

Crew's Corner had gasoline pumps for the duster planes that were used to spray the crops. This was located on Lexington Avenue and Gallatin Road, which are now Santa Anita Avenue and Garvey Boulevard.

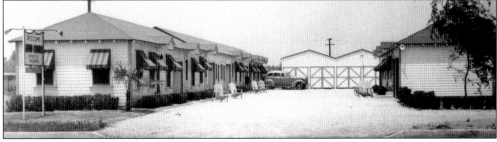

Located on Garvey Boulevard near Five Points, this typical auto court was very popular during the 1930s as people traveled across the country. Each room had cooking facilities and a garage to park their car in at night. When modern motels and hotels were built, people would rent these auto courts by the month.

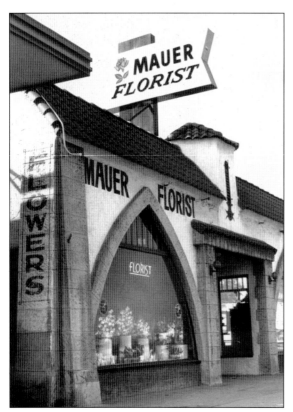

The Mauer Flower Shop, originated by Mary and William Mauer in the 1930s, was located on Garvey Boulevard and Washington Avenue. Two generations ran it with the slogan, "Say it With Flowers, Buy them at Mauers."

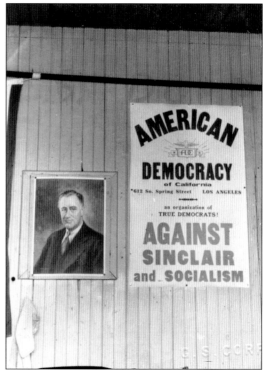

In late 1934, Franklin Delano Roosevelt supporters had an office on Valley Boulevard in El Monte.

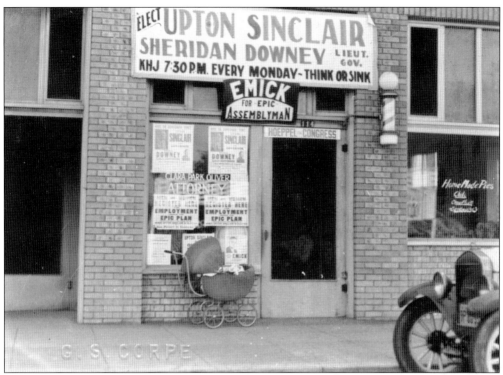

Before the election of November 6, 1934, Upton Sinclair had his office on 114 Valley Boulevard next to Esses' Café.

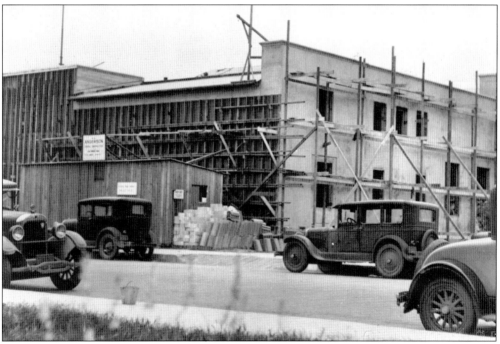

The construction of the post office in 1935 was a big event in town. It was located on Lexington Avenue just north of the El Monte City School District Office.

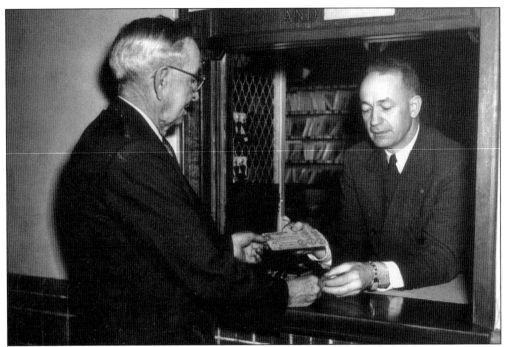

Pictured here is postmaster Thomas J. Caffrey selling the first $25 United States saving bond in El Monte during World War II to Tom Lambert, a realtor in town. Caffrey, appointed by Franklin Delano Roosevelt as postmaster in 1934, had previously served El Monte as mayor and councilman.

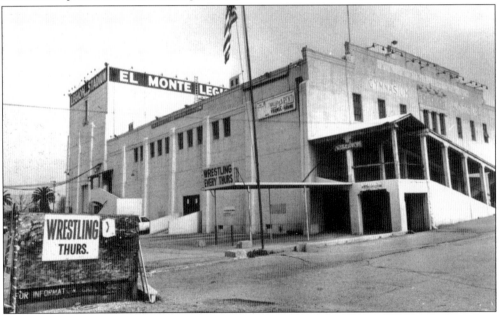

The El Monte American Legion Post 261, organized in 1924, purchased the old high school stadium and auditorium in the early 1940s. Its 160,000 square feet made it ideal for events involving large crowds. Legion Stadium is best remembered as the place for dancing to the music of Tennessee Ernie Ford, Mollie Bee, Cliffie Stone, and, in the 1950s and 1960s, various rock-and-roll acts. The two things most associate with El Monte are Gay's Lion Farm and the Legion Stadium.

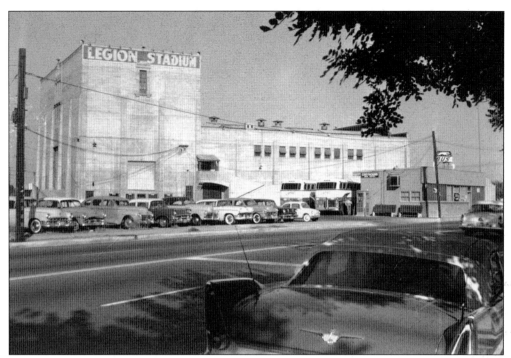

Musical entertainment continued at the Legion Stadium throughout the 1960s, along with boxing, wrestling, roller derbies, and even a circus. In the 1970s, the stadium was sold to the U.S. government and torn down to build the present-day post office.

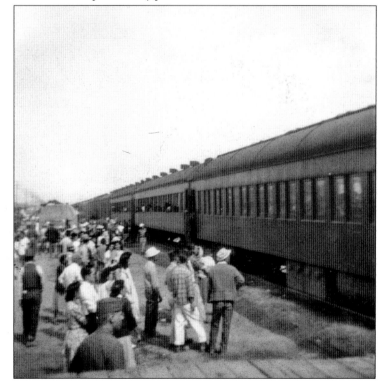

In 1942, the El Monte Japanese were sent to an internment camp at Heart Mountain, Wyoming. They began their stay at Santa Anita Race Track where some El Monte High School students tried to visit them but were not allowed to enter to the camp.

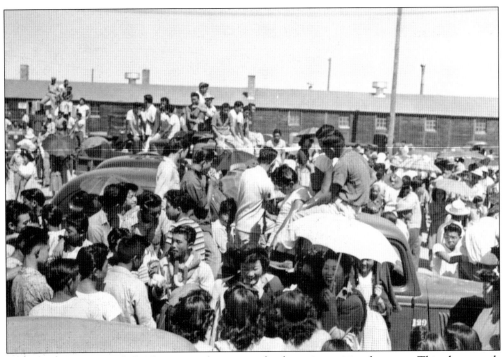

It became a waiting game for the interned—waiting for the train, waiting for a tent. This photograph was taken at Heart Mountain in August 1943.

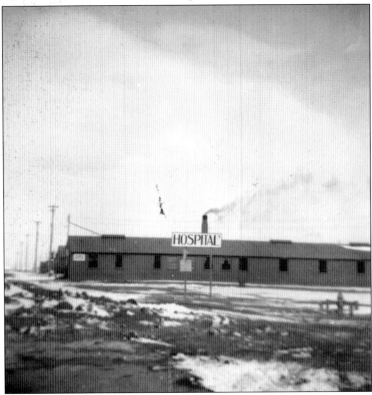

Here are the barracks and hospital at the Heart Mountain internment camp in 1942; it was bleak and snowy. Southern Californians were hardly used to this.

These friends are in an unfamiliar location in Wyoming.

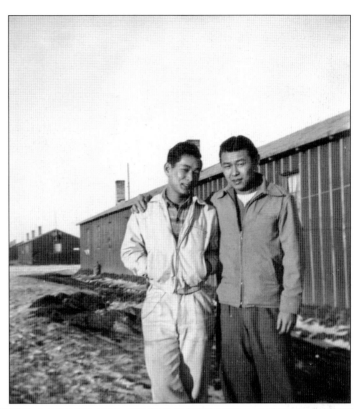

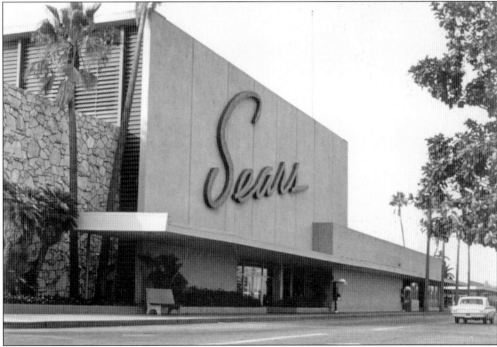

The civic leaders were pleased when Sears came to town. It has since left this building, having relocated in town.

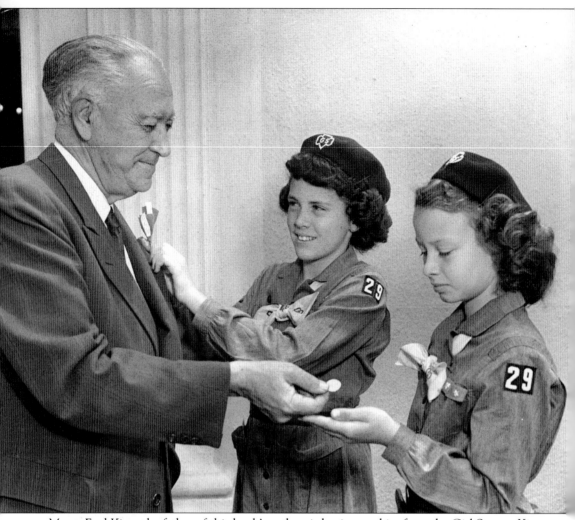
Mayor Fred King, the father of this book's author, is buying cookies from the Girl Scouts. King was the first city manager of El Monte.

In 1925, Ruth K. Kerr became superintendent of the Ruth Home, a charitable institution caring for unmarried mothers and their babies. She sponsored and helped raise funds to build a hospital, house, and school for the Ruth Home. Her husband, Alexander H. Kerr Sr., founder of the glass company that bears his name, helped fund this and other charitable activities.

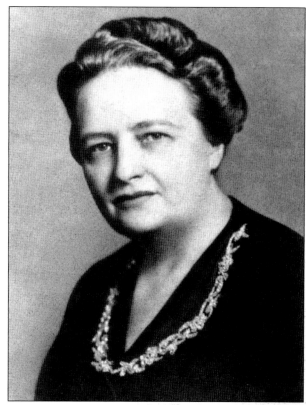

This is the front entrance to the Ruth Home on the east side, just off Gillman Road.

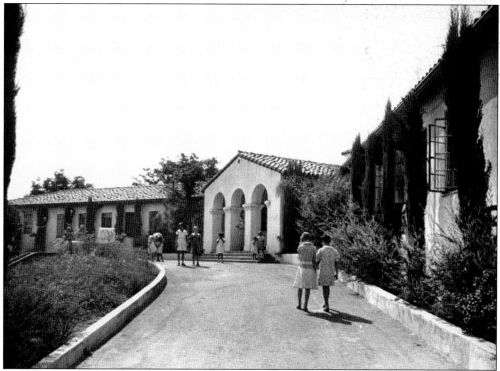

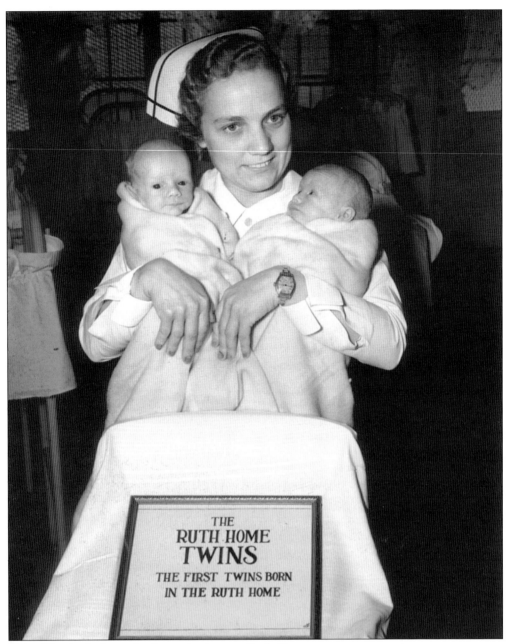

Nurse Klotzback shows the first twins born at Ruth Home.

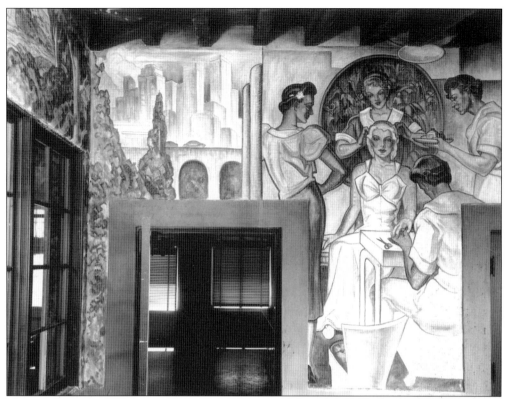
This art deco mural at the main entrance of the Ruth Home features young ladies.

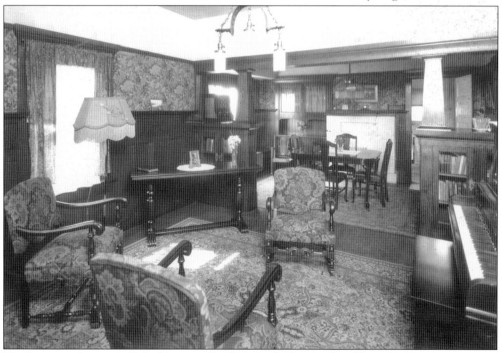
The home study room off the library at Ruth Home had a comfortable ambience to it.

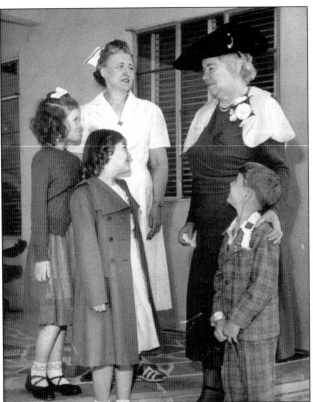

The Ruth Home became the Sister Kenny Polio Hospital in the 1940s when the polio epidemic spread in the United States. This photograph was taken in 1942, before the clinic opened in El Monte.

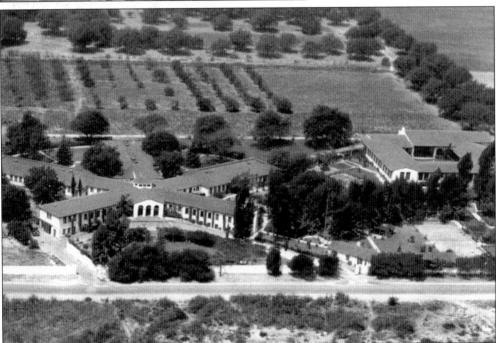

The Ruth Home became the Sister Elizabeth Kenny Polio Hospital and later McClaren Hall, which was run by Los Angeles County for the care of minors.

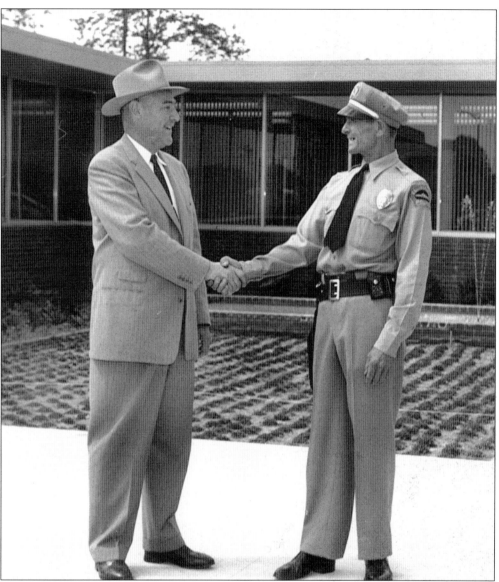
Edwin M. Wiggins, outgoing chief of police, shakes hands with the new chief, Jay Sherman, in October 1956.

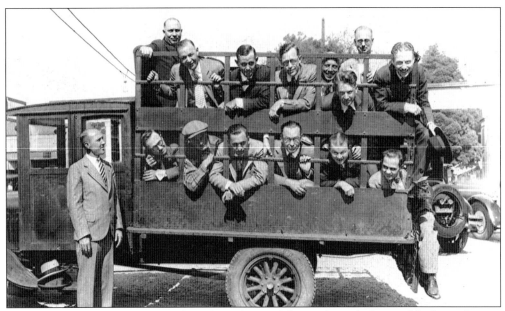
Members of the Lions Club take a fun ride in this Model T Ford Truck. Some of the better known citizens here are Dr. Valentine, dentist; Frank Wright, school superintendent; Guy McMichael, postmaster; and Neil Murray, editor of the El Monte Herald.

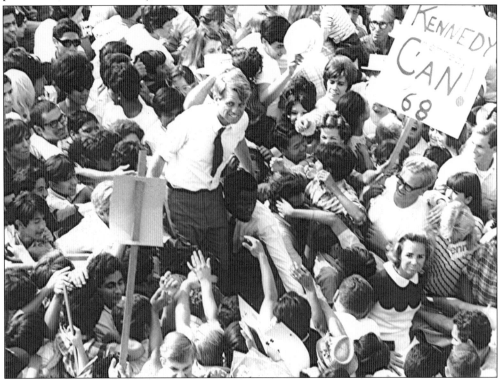
Robert Kennedy passed through El Monte in June 1968, the same month he was shot by an assassin's bullet. He was at the Ambassador Hotel in Los Angeles on June 6 celebrating his California primary win for the Democratic nomination for the presidency of the United States.

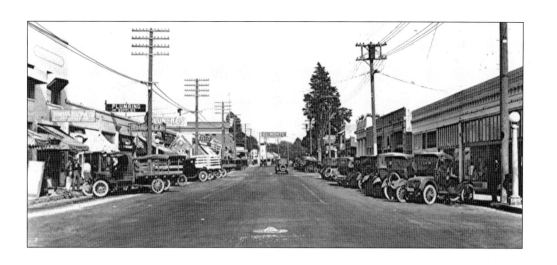

Goodbye for now El Monte.

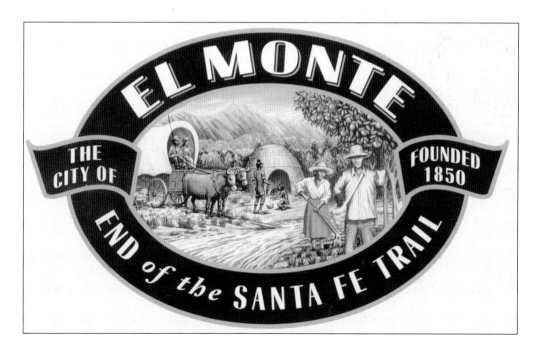

Across America, People are Discovering Something Wonderful. Their Heritage.

Arcadia Publishing is the leading local history publisher in the United States. With more than 3,000 titles in print and hundreds of new titles released every year, Arcadia has extensive specialized experience chronicling the history of communities and celebrating America's hidden stories, bringing to life the people, places, and events from the past. To discover the history of other communities across the nation, please visit:

www.arcadiapublishing.com

Customized search tools allow you to find regional history books about the town where you grew up, the cities where your friends and family live, the town where your parents met, or even that retirement spot you've been dreaming about.

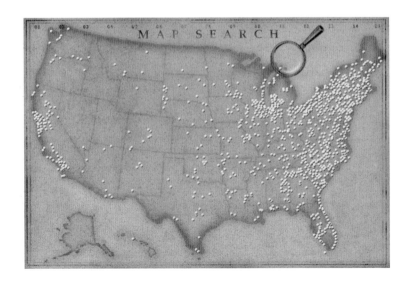